A Short Primer on Innovative Evaluation Reporting

by Kylie Hutchinson

National Library of Canada Cataloguing in Publication

Hutchinson, Kylie, 1966 –
        A Short Primer on Innovative Evaluation Reporting.

ISBN 978-0-9952774-1-0

First edition, 2017

Illustrations by Chris Lysy at www.freshspectrum.com.

Copies of this book may be purchased from www.communitysolutions.ca.

For more information contact:
Kylie Hutchinson
Community Solutions Planning & Evaluation
PO Box 1911
Gibsons, BC, V0N 1V0
Canada
604-243-9458
www.communitysolutions.ca

About the Author

Kylie Hutchinson took her first course in evaluation in 1988 and was forever hooked. After winning the Canadian Evaluation Society's Student Competition and several years working for nonprofits, she leaped into evaluation consulting. For many years she delivered the Canadian Evaluation Society's Essential Skills Series in British Columbia and continues to provide training on a variety of evaluation topics for clients such as the American Evaluation Association, Canadian Evaluation Society, African Evaluation Society, Danish Evaluation Society, and the US Centres for Disease Control. Kylie has a passion for translating evaluation theory into practical products for evaluators in the trenches. Over the years she has produced a variety of free evaluation resources including tip sheets, a podcast, whiteboard videos, a mobile learning course for senior decision-makers, and an online evaluation glossary. In 2016, she published her first guidebook for nonprofits, *Survive and Thrive: Three Steps to Securing Your Program's Sustainability*. Kylie regularly contributes to the AEA365 blog and tweets regularly on evaluation topics at @EvaluationMaven.

Acknowledgements

I would like to thank Carolyn Camman, Lesley Dyck, Sheila B. Robinson, Echo Rivera, Kate Svensson, and Hannah Pickar for their valuable feedback on the initial manuscript. Thank you to all the individuals and organizations who granted me permission to use their examples and images. Thank you to Mark Cameron for coming through when I really needed it. Special thanks to Chris Lysy for making his cartoons available and for generally keeping all of us in the evaluation profession laughing.

To Mike and Lucy

Table of Contents

Introduction

In 2008, I unexpectedly discovered there was a better way for me to do my evaluation reports. Let me tell you how.

I had just finished giving a great slide presentation to a client of mine, where I summarized the results of an evaluation I conducted for their organization. I was very excited about the results, and even more excited about the subsequent program and policy change that I envisioned occurring afterward. After my presentation, the program coordinator thanked me for my work, and I left feeling pretty good. On my way home from their office, I shared a seat on a commuter bus with a woman who lived in the same neighborhood as me. We chatted for a bit then both went back to our reading. But I couldn't help glancing at the open book she had on her lap. The book was mostly images. They were bold, colorful, and grabbed my attention immediately. It took only moments for me to realize that it was a book about slide design. As I peered over the woman's shoulder, the pages piqued my curiosity and I asked her if I could take a quick look. I quickly flipped through the book (called *Presentation Zen*[1]), wrapping my head around the author's message. With my stomach in a minor free fall, the full realization hit me - the standards for presentation slides had changed significantly and I was guilty of bad slide design. The "great" presentation I had just given turned out to be not so great at all. In fact, it was possibly quite boring and probably forgettable. And if it was boring and forgettable, how likely was it that my audience would remember the content and implement my recommendations? I suddenly thought about the final report I had also prepared. My heart sank thinking about the thirty-nine pages of single-spaced text contained within. Would they find that boring and forgettable as well?

When my neighbor offered to lend me the book for a few days, I jumped at the chance. It was a quick read, and I was nearly finished before I got off the bus. Arriving home, I was so excited about what I learned I immediately showed it to my husband. He took the book, leafed through it briefly, then slammed it shut. "No! I can't!" he said in a panic, "I have to make a presentation tomorrow at 9 am, and I don't have time to change my slides! Take it away! Aaauuughhh!" And then he stayed up half the night changing them anyway.

I'm an evaluation consultant who works mostly with nonprofits. I took my first evaluation course in 1988 and went out on my own as an

My "great" presentation was not so great after all.

How much thought and consideration do we give to how we deliver our results?

independent consultant in 1997. I'd done many evaluations and made many presentations to clients. But I had never thought much about how I delivered my results. As the days went by I started thinking more about our profession and how we traditionally present our evaluation findings in a lengthy report. I decided I wanted to share what I had learned with other evaluators so I submitted a workshop proposal for that year's American Evaluation Association conference on the broader topic of evaluation reporting. To my delight, it was accepted. I was nervous delivering my first pre-conference workshop, but I was also pretty sure I'd have a receptive audience for my message. As evaluators, we pride ourselves on putting effort and expertise into conducting quality evaluations. But how much thought and consideration do we give to how we deliver our results? The workshop feedback turned out to be very positive, and years later I continue to bring the message of more innovative reporting to evaluators.

Now I've summarized this workshop into a concise guide for evaluators like you. Evaluators who feel their final reports just aren't hitting the mark. Evaluators who wish to better engage their stakeholders through their reports. Evaluators who wish to see their findings appropriately used.

What's Inside

This book is a short primer on why and how to improve your evaluation reports. It is not solely about slide design, and neither is it a detailed review of the literature on evaluation utilization or the neuroscience behind data visualization and communications. It is a quick and practical introduction (or a refresher) on why reporting matters in evaluation with simple principles and ideas for how to make your reports more engaging. When you are finished reading, I hope you will feel inspired to try something new and innovative, all in the name of greater utilization.

In Chapter 1, I briefly discuss why our field needs to re-think the traditional-style long report. In Chapter 2, I introduce four principles that will immediately improve your reporting practice. Chapter 3 summarizes how to craft key messages that are "sticky" and inspire action. In Chapter 4, since many of you work in environments where a long report is still mandatory, I discuss common report errors along with some simple ideas for making them more engaging. In Chapter 5, I present several alternatives that you can use instead of, or in addition to, the traditional report. In Chapter 6, I offer suggestions on how to implement these techniques in your workplace. Throughout the book, you'll find real-life examples plus numerous tips for effective execution.

What are you waiting for? Dive in, and see how your evaluation reports can go from *ho-hum* to *awesome*.

Chapter 1 - Why Reporting Matters

Reporting your results is one of the most important tasks of an evaluator, but doing it in an engaging way that inspires action is often neglected. Consider the typical program cycle below. Many of you will likely be familiar with this image in one form or another. Moving clockwise, it starts with an assessment of current needs. This is followed by the design of an intervention or program to meet those needs, the implementation of the program, and at some point, an evaluation. We assume the results of the evaluation will inform changes to the program design and operations and the cycle will continue.

Unfortunately, this doesn't always happen. Instead, we've been taught to place our evaluation findings into a lengthy final report that often gets ignored. To be honest, I'm convinced that a great many of these long reports end up in a black hole somewhere. There is rarely uptake of recommendations, no lessons learned, and most importantly, no program improvement.

LEARNING OBJECTIVE

After reading this chapter, you will be able to:

• Describe the role that effective reporting plays in good evaluation practice.

Typical Program Cycle

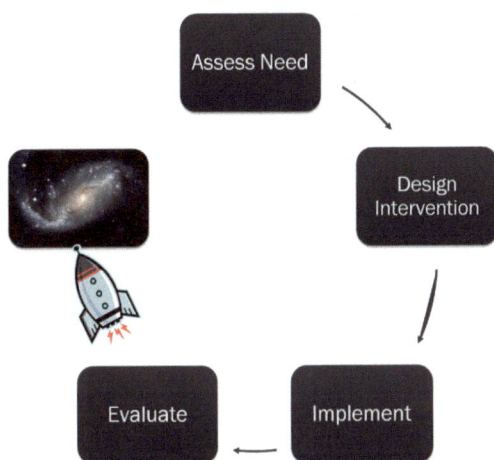

Often our reports end up in a black hole somewhere.

People don't read long reports.

Why does this happen? Here's my theory, and it's not a pretty one. People don't read long reports.

"Your final report is deep and wide.
I almost drowned while reading it."

Source: ©2008 Reprinted with permission from Patrick Hardin.

REFLECT

Think about your own workload right now.
How tall is the stack of reading on your
to-do list (hard copy and electronic)?

a) 1 inch

b) 1 foot

c) I'm ashamed to tell you

d) I thought that was a plant stand!

Think about it. How tall is the stack of reading in your inbox right now? I'm referring to hard copy documents piled up in your office plus all those electronic PDFs sitting in your email. Most of us have a heap of reading that we're "going to get to someday." The problem is that someday often never comes. What is relevant one day gets (literally) buried over time by new projects, new directives, and new areas of interest. Before we know it, months or even years have passed, and the innocent pile of reading in the corner has turned into a monster that prevents us from shutting the office door. Despite our best intentions, what we were once determined to read now seems irrelevant.

Eventually, in an attempt to simplify our lives and lessen our guilt, we do a spring cleaning and end up recycling most of this reading or deleting it from our inbox. It feels great, but do you ever worry about what gets tossed out? Think about why you set aside those reports in the first place. There must have been something that you believed would inform a project, add to your knowledge base, or generally make you better at what you do. But now they're gone, along with any potential insights that might have been inside. As someone who has been at the other end diligently writing those reports, it makes me want to cry. All that hard work, for nothing.

Indeed, it's for this very reason that I intentionally designed this book to be relatively short. If I made it too long, you might not have time to read it yourself, or be able to find specific information you need easily.

Politicians and Reading

How much time do you think policymakers have to read your documents? One study of US senior National Security decision makers found that the biggest challenge they face in assimilating scholarly or other reports is lack of time.[2] I also found an old statistic that back in 1977 members of the US House of Representatives spent an average of 11 minutes per day reading.[3] I wonder how substantially their volume of reading has increased since then? Several local politicians I know have personally told me that staying on top of their reading is one of the biggest challenges of their job. I can only imagine this would be similar for senior decision makers and policy makers in other organizations. How do we capture the attention of these busy individuals who are ultimately responsible for using the evidence we produce?

Drowning in Information

These days we all suffer from information overload. Every day, all day long, we are bombarded with information through any number of channels. Our lengthy evaluation reports are part of this problem, but what can we do? As evaluators, we are duty-bound to report on our results.

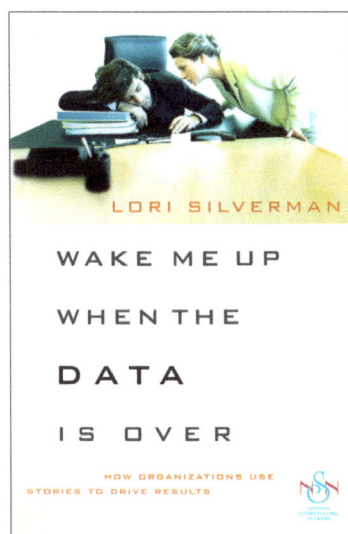

LORI SILVERMAN

WAKE ME UP

WHEN THE

DATA

IS OVER

HOW ORGANIZATIONS USE STORIES TO DRIVE RESULTS

This is the title of a real book![4]

> **...we have long known that the primary constraint policymakers face in digesting scholarly, or any other writings, is lack of time.**
>
> Paul Avey and Michael Desch[2]

Think about the implications if our reports aren't read. Occasionally, I do strategic planning for nonprofits, and before a session, I ask to see copies of any evaluations they have conducted in the past few years. They often ask me why, and it shocks me. If there's one obvious place for evaluation to drive change, it's through an organization's strategic planning process. But all too often these evaluations and the recommendations for action contained within are absent from the planning table. We often talk about "lessons learned" but if no one is reading our reports, is anything truly learned? I suspect that more often than not we keep making the same mistakes.

Do You Read Fast Enough?

According to a speed reading test sponsored by a major office retailer, the average person reads at a rate of 300 words per minute. Higher-educated individuals, such as business executives, read at a speed of 475 words per minute, and college professors read at 675. Given that one page of a typical evaluation report (single-spaced, 12 pt. font) is 500 words, our intended users require approximately one minute per page to read our final reports. Fifty-page report: fifty minutes of reading. Simple enough, no?

Now consider that our evaluation report is not the only piece of reading on their plate. There's also email, meeting agendas and minutes, work briefs, blog posts, the newspaper, and other reading for research and professional development. In a 2012 article in Forbes magazine, Brett Nelson estimates that the average executive requires an hour of reading a day just to keep up.[5] While that might not sound bad, consider how this can add up over a month. That's almost three days a month! How many managers do you know who are realistically able to devote this amount of time to their reading?

If you'd like to test your own reading speed, try http://www.freereadingtest.com.

Ideal Program Cycle

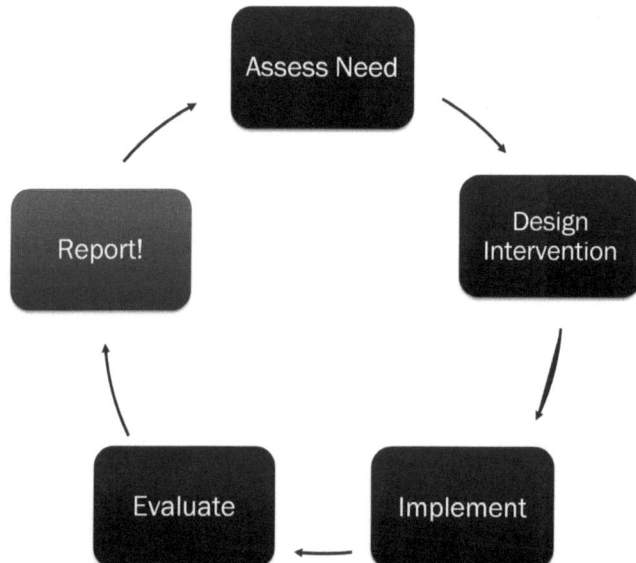

Imagine if reporting was a recognized part of the program cycle.

Confidence in Charities

In 2015, the Chronicle of Philanthropy conducted a survey that found that thirty-five percent of the American public had little or no confidence in charities.[6] And it's not just in the US. Similar research in the UK found that trust and confidence in charities has fallen to the lowest recorded level since monitoring began in 2005.[7]

When I first came across these numbers, I was shocked. Over the years, I've worked with dozens of charitable organizations. On the whole, I've seen some amazing work performed and impacts achieved. Although my experience is mostly in the Canadian context, I'm willing to bet the effectiveness of US and UK charities does not differ significantly. But if these achievements are buried in a report somewhere, it's possible to see why the public persists in believing their donations are not being spent effectively.

Imagine how different things would be if our evaluation reports were fully read. What if every program cycle formally incorporated "Report and Encourage Utilization" as one stage of the cycle (similar to the figure to the left). When I first started researching evaluation use, I learned that our field has been struggling with this issue for years, as evidenced by articles that go back as far as 1978. Of course, there are other factors that influence utilization beyond reporting, but I think you'll agree that how we communicate our findings plays a substantial role.

At this point, I have a confession to make. I hate writing evaluation reports.

There, I said it. I know, I know, I'm an evaluator, but I still hate writing reports. It's my least favorite part of the evaluation process. Logic models? Love 'em. Engaging stakeholders? Bring it on. Designing surveys? I could do it all day long. Analyzing data? I'm swooning. But writing the final report? Ugh. I suspect some of you might feel the same. When I learned from well-known evaluator, Michael Quinn Patton, that between 25% and 30% of an evaluator's time is spent writing a final report, I shook my head in bewilderment.[8] Why are we spending so much time on something that frequently doesn't get read beyond the executive summary?

I don't know about you, but I rarely have the evaluation budget available to do the evaluation I really want to do. If you gave me another 30% to spend, I could immediately think of several valuable ways to spend the additional funds. I could consult more stakeholders,

When is an Evaluation Finished?

You may laugh at the cartoon below, but this used to be a consulting dilemma of mine. As an independent consultant with projects lasting months and sometimes years, I learned pretty quickly that I wasn't going to get paid every two weeks. The day I finished a project and could finally send my invoice was a happy one. The problem was, when exactly was I finished? I used to think it was immediately after I had delivered the final report. Several years later I attended a workshop with Michael Quinn Patton who mentioned that our job as evaluators doesn't end when we deliver the final report. In his opinion, if we are truly concerned about evaluation use, we should try to spend another three to six months working with the program to encourage the uptake and use of the findings. I still struggle with when to send my final invoice, but now I accept that my role as an evaluator doesn't end once I've submitted a final report.

Keep trying! You can make sure the results get used! There's still hope! Try to improve the program! Don't let your hard work go to waste!

This is just business. Just send your client that boring evaluation report and call it a day. Don't worry about it.

@AnnKEmery & freshspectrum.com

increase the amount of data collected, or tap into additional lines of evidence. Instead, this money is often wasted on writing a long report that people don't read. Think of the missed potential. Nowadays, I'll share this piece of information with programs I'm evaluating and ask them what they prefer: a formal report or a two-page summary with the balance applied to other evaluation activities. The majority of my evaluation clients now opt for a short report.

The Challenge

Here's our challenge as evaluators: We need to take messy data and package it in a way that makes it sticky in the minds of managers and other decision makers who use our findings to improve programs, develop policy, and generally make things better. By sticky I mean something that users are able to easily recall and act on when the time comes. The problem is when we deliver our long reports, months or even years might pass before users find themselves in a position to take action on the results. It's highly unlikely for a decision maker to read an evaluation report then immediately turn around and step into a meeting to develop policy. Or if they do, they've often only read the executive summary. The lag time between when a stakeholder first reads our recommendations and when they can actually implement them can be lengthy. Unfortunately, we often only get one chance to communicate our findings, particularly if we're an external evaluator.

Our job is to ensure that when the time for action does come, these managers are able to recall our major findings and recommendations, so they can implement program or policy change. We need to start thinking outside the inbox because the standard final report is not serving us, nor the people who need the evidence we produce, very well. We need to move from the traditional lengthy final report to something that actually effects change for the people, communities, and environment we care about.

If we adopt more innovative forms of reporting, what's in it for us as evaluators? It's knowing that our findings won't be lost in a black hole. It's viewing concrete change that arises from our evaluation results, and seeing how we're tangibly making a difference with our work, every day. In fact, as you'll see throughout this primer, the reporting concepts I discuss fall into more than one of the *Program Evaluation Standards* on Utility:

U2 Attention to Stakeholders—Evaluations should devote attention to the full range of individuals and groups invested in the program and affected by its evaluation.

U5 Relevant Information—Evaluation information should serve the identified and emergent needs of stakeholders.

U6 Meaningful Processes and Products—Evaluations should construct activities, descriptions, and judgments in ways that encourage participants to rediscover, reinterpret, or revise their understandings and behaviors.

U7 Timely and Appropriate Communicating and Reporting—Evaluations should attend to the continuing information needs of their multiple audiences.[9]

> **The standard final report is not serving us, nor the people who need the evidence we produce, very well.**

Evaluation, Reporting, and Program Sustainability

Evaluation results are a great way to raise the profile of an organization's work. In my experience, many of the evaluations I conduct reflect excellent and successful initiatives delivered by highly competent staff. But I'm always surprised at how infrequently these positive results are used by organizations for their own public relations and marketing purposes. Having a high organizational profile is associated with greater program sustainability in the nonprofit literature.[10] But if these good news stories are buried in a lengthy report, the organization misses an opportunity to raise their profile and reinforce their long-term sustainability at the same time. By using more innovative and powerful reporting techniques, we can assist the programs we evaluate to find a wider audience for their results beyond their internal staff.

By now I hope you'll agree that we all need to rethink our dependence on the lengthy final report. Even if we can't or don't want to get rid of it entirely, there should be options for communicating our findings in a way that encourages greater uptake and use. In fact, there are many, which I'll begin to describe in the next chapter.

Chapter Summary

- Busy decision makers have limited time to read lengthy reports.

- If evaluation reports aren't read, there is inadequate uptake of recommendations, less program improvement, and most importantly, few lessons learned.

- The lag time between when a decision maker first reads a recommendation and when they can actually implement program or policy change can be lengthy. We need to make our findings easy to recall and act on when the time comes.

- How we communicate our findings plays a significant role in evaluation utilization and concrete change.

Chapter 2 - Principles for More Effective Reporting

I f we're going to improve our reporting practice, we need some guidelines. Here are four principles for more effective reporting:

Target Your Audience

Develop a Communications Plan

Layer Your Content

Reorder Your Key Messages

LEARNING OBJECTIVE

After reading this chapter, you will be able to:

• State four principles for effectively communicating your results.

Let's look at each in detail.

Target Your Audience

The evaluation profession could learn a thing or two from marketing and communications, and this is one of them. Every marketer recognizes the importance of audience segmentation, and we should too. Often the goal of presenting our findings is to persuade an audience to adopt our results. But it's important to recognize that different stakeholders have different information needs, and the typical one-size-fits-all style of the standard report serves these unique audiences poorly. While a decision-maker might be looking for high-level policy implications, a program manager will be more interested in concrete ways to improve the program. Program staff may be interested in feedback from participants, while funders will be looking for evidence of outcomes. Diverse stakeholders might also view the effectiveness of a program in varying ways. What is perceived as highly successful by participants might be considered marginal by funders.

Who is Your Audience?

Every evaluation report has several different audiences, namely the evaluation stakeholders. Stakeholders are "individuals or groups served by, affected by, or with a legitimate interest in the program or the evaluation."[11] Who are typical stakeholders in an evaluation? They might include:

- staff
- managers and coordinators
- participants
- funders

- senior executives
- board members
- policy makers
- the general public

Having a sense of who your stakeholders are can help target your audience.

Factors That Influence Evaluation Use

In 2009, evaluators Dreolin Fletcher and Christina Christie surveyed American Evaluation Association members to determine their opinions on what practices exert the most influence on evaluation use.[12] As you can see from the figure below, eighty-six percent of respondents indicated "Identifying and prioritizing intended users of the evaluation" was either "Influential" or "Extremely influential."

Identifying intended users and **communication** figure strongly in factors that influence evaluation use.

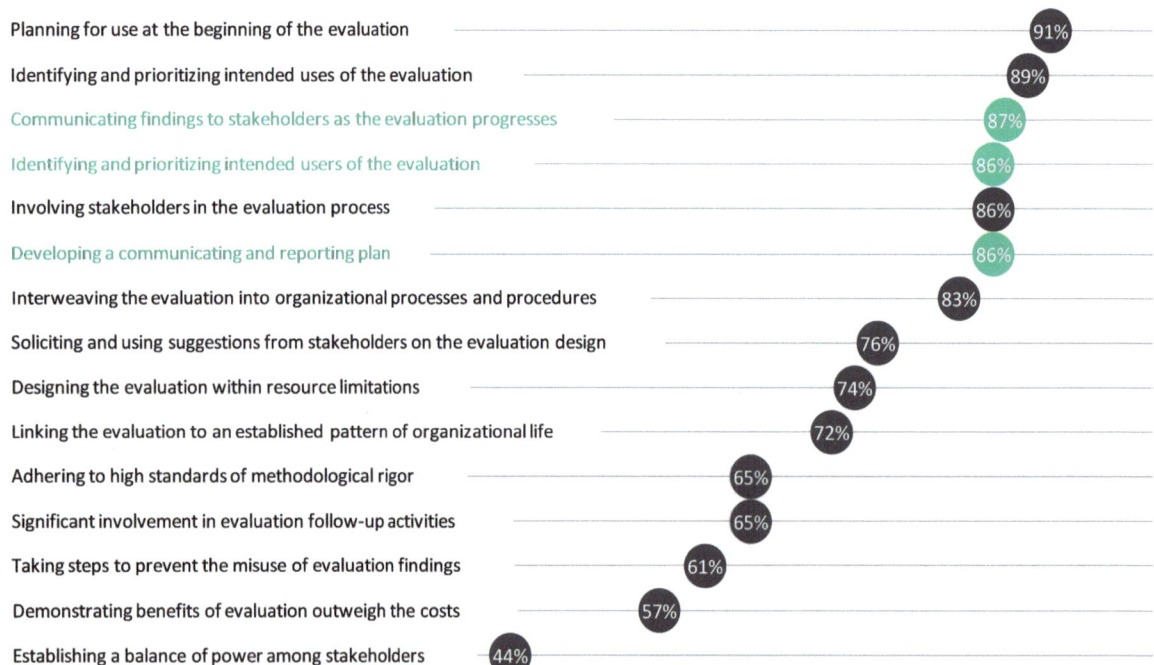

Factor	%
Planning for use at the beginning of the evaluation	91%
Identifying and prioritizing intended uses of the evaluation	89%
Communicating findings to stakeholders as the evaluation progresses	87%
Identifying and prioritizing intended users of the evaluation	86%
Involving stakeholders in the evaluation process	86%
Developing a communicating and reporting plan	86%
Interweaving the evaluation into organizational processes and procedures	83%
Soliciting and using suggestions from stakeholders on the evaluation design	76%
Designing the evaluation within resource limitations	74%
Linking the evaluation to an established pattern of organizational life	72%
Adhering to high standards of methodological rigor	65%
Significant involvement in evaluation follow-up activities	65%
Taking steps to prevent the misuse of evaluation findings	61%
Demonstrating benefits of evaluation outweigh the costs	57%
Establishing a balance of power among stakeholders	44%

Stakeholder groups have distinct preferences for how they wish to receive the results. For example, program staff may want to meet in-person for a detailed review, while busy senior executives might only have time to read a one-page briefing note. What is appropriate for a board member might not be suitable for participants with literacy issues. If you can identify your different stakeholder groups, you can tailor the content and style of your reports to their specific concerns. Notice I used the plural, "reports." You'll likely need more than one type of communication format to reach these diverse audiences. This might sound like a lot of work, but you likely already do this and don't realize it. For example, have you ever prepared a tailored presentation for a board of directors in addition to the final report? Or have you ever shortened a final presentation so you could present it during a committee meeting?

In order to reach all of ourdiverse audiences, the final report is now 17,000 pages.

You can pick it up here. Hand-trucks are available at the back of the room.

freshspectrum.com

Identifying your stakeholders is more than just making a list. You need to consider in what ways they are different so you can appropriately target the content, key messages, and communication format. Where and how do they prefer to receive new information? What language level is the most appropriate? What tone is best: formal or folksy? What do you want them to do with the information? Increase their understanding or advocate for a particular decision? Again, you likely do this already when you consider what to present to program staff versus the program participants.

Targeting Your Audience

Source: © 2006 Reprinted with permission from Nettie Wild.

Years ago, I evaluated a pilot health promotion intervention involving the British Columbia Centre for Disease Control's (BCCDC) Outreach Street Nurse Program. The outreach street nurses provide sexually transmitted infection, HIV, and tuberculosis prevention services for vulnerable populations. For several years, the rates of syphilis had been climbing among street-involved individuals in Vancouver, BC's Downtown Eastside including injection drug users, sexually-exploited women, and street-involved youth. To respond, the BCCDC launched an innovative but controversial intervention they called the Syphilis Blitz. The blitz involved shifting their outreach street nurses and other health care workers from their regular duties to distribute antibiotics to all residents, infected or not, in the affected neighborhood for a two-week period. The idea was to interrupt the trajectory of the disease through an intensive spread of antibiotics thus increasing the resistance of the community as a whole. The street nurses involved were very concerned about the blitz. They were uncomfortable with the mass distribution of antibiotics and they worried about how the blitz would affect their relationship with clients. The evaluation findings, however, were surprising. The vast majority of individuals taking the antibiotics said the blitz actually increased their respect and appreciation of the street nurses.

When it came time to report the findings, I realized I had three distinct audiences:

• BCCDC senior managers

• the street nurses

• individuals taking the medication

For the busy senior managers, I prepared a short two-page briefing note. For the street nurses, I held a data party (see *Data Parties*) where I presented the draft results and asked for input on my initial conclusions and recommendations. I chose a data party in particular because of the degree to which my findings conflicted with their previous assumptions. I wanted the nurses to have sufficient time to question and understand the findings. Finally, for the individuals taking the antibiotics, I posted two flip charts that summarized the main results in the waiting room of the neighborhood medical clinic so they could review them as they waited for their appointment. And it was worth it. Each of these three distinct communication methods worked so well I can't imagine having done it any other way.

Nancy Duarte, a well-known communications and presentation design expert, has seven questions she suggests asking to better understand your audience in the figure to the right.

Data Parties

A data party is an occasion for stakeholders to review and interact with an evaluation's initial findings before you draft a final report. Also known as a sense-making session or participatory data analysis, data parties give stakeholders the opportunity to actively analyze the data and offer their own interpretations. They also allow stakeholders to provide input into appropriate conclusions and recommendations, thereby increasing buy-in for later implementation. (See *Data Parties* in the Appendix.)

You can hold a data party with a small group of program staff or a large community gathering. They usually require a minimum of two to three hours and are led by an evaluator or another individual who is comfortable with group facilitation. To learn more about specific activities to use during a data party, check out Public Profit's publication, *Dabbling in the Data: A Hands-on Guide to Participatory Data Analysis.*[13]

Seven Questions to Knowing Your Audience

Insert a representative picture or illustration of an audience member in this rectangle. It helps to put a face on the audience.

1 What are they like?

Demographics and psychographics are a great start, but connecting with your audience means understanding them on a personal level. Take a walk in their shoes and describe what their life looks like each day.

2 Why are they here?

What do they think they're going to get out of this presentation? Why did they come to hear you? Are they willing participants or mandatory attendees? This is also a bit of a situation analysis.

3 What keeps them up at night?

Everyone has a fear, a pain point, a thorn in the side. Let your audience know you empathize—and offer a solution.

4 How can you solve their problem?

What's in it for the audience? How are you going to make their lives better?

5 What do you want them to do?

Answer the question "so what?"—and make sure there's clear action for your audience to take.

6 How can you best reach them?

People vary in how they receive information. This can include the set up of the room to the availability of materials after the presentation. Give the audience what they want, how they want it.

7 How might they resist?

What will keep them from adopting your message and carrying out your call to action?

© duarte.com 2008

These seven questions can help you better target your audience.[14]

GET TO KNOW YOUR EVALUATION STAKEHOLDERS

YOU'VE IDENTIFIED YOUR POTENTIAL STAKEHOLDERS, **NOW WHAT?** GET THEIR INPUT BY ASKING SOME OF THE FOLLOWING QUESTIONS...

WHAT DO THEY PERCEIVE THE PURPOSE OF YOUR PROGRAM IS?

WHAT IS THEIR CURRENT OPINION OF THE PROGRAM?

WHAT CONCERNS, IF ANY, DO THEY HAVE ABOUT THE PROGRAM?

WHAT INFLUENCES THEIR OPINION OF THE PROGRAM, AND/OR THEIR OPINIONS GENERALLY?

WHAT HAVE THEY HEARD ABOUT THE PROPOSED PROGRAM EVALUATION?

WHAT AREAS DO THEY THINK ARE IMPORTANT TO ADDRESS FIRST IN THE EVALUATION?

WHAT DO THEY HOPE TO LEARN FROM THE EVALUATION?

HOW MUCH PROGRESS DO THEY THINK IS REASONABLE TO EXPECT FOR THIS PROGRAM AT THIS TIME?

WHAT CONCERNS, IF ANY, DO THEY HAVE WITH THE PROGRAM EVALUATION?

WHAT FINANCIAL OR EMOTIONAL INTEREST DO THEY HAVE IN THE OUTCOME OF THE EVALUATION? IS IT POSITIVE OR NEGATIVE?

IF THEY ARE NOT LIKELY TO BE POSITIVE WHAT WILL WIN THEM AROUND? OR IF YOU ARE UNLIKELY TO WIN THEM AROUND, HOW WILL YOU MANAGE THEIR OPPOSITION?

HOW AVAILABLE ARE THEY TO PARTICIPATE IN THE EVALUATION PROCESS?

WHAT RESOURCES (I.E., TIME, FUNDS, EVALUATION EXPERTISE, ACCESS TO RESPONDENTS, ACCESS TO POLICYMAKERS) MIGHT THEY CONTRIBUTE?

WHAT SUPPORT DO YOU WANT FROM THEM?

WHAT ARE THE POLITICAL IMPLICATIONS OF THEIR INVOLVEMENT IN THE EVALUATION?

HOW WILL THEY USE THE RESULTS OF THIS EVALUATION? WHAT DECISIONS ARE GOING TO BE MADE BY WHOM, AND WHEN?

HOW CAN YOU BEST MEET THEIR COMMUNICATION NEEDS? WHAT INFORMATION DO THEY WANT FROM YOU?

HOW DO THEY WANT TO RECEIVE THIS INFORMATION? WHAT IS THE BEST WAY OF COMMUNICATING WITH THEM?

Community Solutions
Planning & Evaluation
www.communitysolutions.ca

Adapted from U.S. Department of Health and Human Services. Centers for Disease Control and Prevention. Office of the Director, Office of Strategy and Innovation. Introduction to program evaluation for public health programs: A self-study guide. Atlanta, GA: Centers for Disease Control and Prevention, 2011, and Salabarría-Peña, Y, Apt, B.S., Walsh, C.M. Practical Use of Program Evaluation among Sexually Transmitted Disease (STD) Programs, Atlanta (GA): Centers for Disease Control and Prevention; 2007.

If you don't know the answers to these questions, it's best not to guess. Instead, ask your stakeholders directly. If you've taken the time to engage them early on in the evaluation, you will already have a good sense of their report preferences. Questions such as those presented in the tip sheet to the left can help inform your actions as you move on to the next three principles of effective reporting.

Develop a Communications Plan

Remember the survey of factors that influence evaluation use I discussed earlier? As you can see from the figure on page 20, eighty-six percent of respondents also identified "Developing a communicating and reporting plan" as either "Influential" or "Extremely influential."

What goes into an evaluation communications plan? While there is no standard format, they usually look something like the example below.

Example Evaluation Communication Plan

Stakeholder	Communication Method	Timing	Budget	Priority
Program Participants	Larger poster in training room	End of evaluation	$$	High
Program Staff	Results-briefings	Interim and end of evaluation	$	High
Senior Managers	Two-page summary	End of evaluation	$	Medium
Funder	Two-page summary Presentation	End of evaluation	$	High
Membership	Article in donor newsletter	Beginning and end of evaluation	$	Medium
Community-at-large	Press release Community forum	Beginning and end of evaluation	$$$$	Medium

Completing the first column, *Stakeholders*, is easy because if you've followed the first principle, Target Your Audience, you'll have identified your different audiences already. If you've taken the time to research their preferences for receiving information, you'll also have an idea of what *Communication Method* is appropriate for the second column. The *Timing* column is important because reporting is not always a one-time event that occurs at the end of an evaluation. It's an ongoing process that begins when the evaluation starts (particularly if you're using a Developmental evaluation approach) and continues, if necessary, beyond the delivery of a final report. In fact, in the AEA survey, evaluators also identified "Communicating findings to stakeholders as the evaluation progresses" as an influential factor. Specifying the timing is also critical because the release of our findings should ideally be scheduled to coincide with major decision-making.

Being cognizant of these windows of opportunity for action can go a long way towards facilitating greater use.

I also recommend including a *Budget* column to ensure you allocate sufficient funds to carry through with your communication plans. I'm often asked how much one should budget overall. Unfortunately, there is no hard and fast rule. While some methods are relatively inexpensive, such as a fact sheet you design yourself, others will require more resources. Some forms of reporting might require talents that are outside of your traditional skill set as an evaluator. Having funds to hire a professional graphic designer or a communication specialist may be necessary.

Finally, I like to include a *Priority* column because so many of us work on projects with limited evaluation funds. If I am not able to follow through with all of my different communication methods, I want to be able to determine which ones I can keep and which I can drop.

This second principle, Develop a Communications Plan, will help you engage with your audiences in a proactive and strategic way.

Layer Your Content

"Layering" is a term I coined in 2008 to describe the simultaneous use of diverse report formats to communicate evaluation results. The purpose of layering is to give stakeholders the option to go as shallow or as deep as they choose into your evaluation findings.

A hamburger makes a great analogy for layering your reporting efforts.

Layering works like this. Consider the standard final report as the meat of a burger. It can be very heavy and take a long time to digest. Final reports are often very dense documents, and not all stakeholders have the time or the appetite to eat them. Sometimes, all they want is a lettuce and tomato salad (e.g., a newsletter), or a slice of cheese (e.g., an infographic). Or they may be rushed and can only take a quick nibble of the bun (e.g., a presentation). While some users will be intrigued enough to eat the whole burger, appendices and all, others might be satisfied with just a few bites.

By offering diverse communication strategies for varying appetites, we give stakeholders the choice of how deeply they want to delve into the results. For example, imagine you are presenting the findings of an evaluation to a steering committee. At the end of the presentation, you give everyone a handout with a URL at the bottom for more information. Afterward, certain committee members wish to know more. Some visit the website, where they read a more detailed synopsis of the evaluation online. Still wanting to learn more, several might download a one-page fact sheet and distribute it at another senior management meeting. At this meeting, there is spirited discussion about moving forward, so plans are made for everyone to read the full report and come to the next meeting prepared to discuss action steps. At this same meeting, someone also asks a detailed question about the methodology used, so a staff person is tasked with downloading the appendices to get the answer.

Layering works because each communication product contains the same key messages and is linked to a more detailed option, enticing the reader to explore more if they choose. Again, not everyone will eat the entire burger, but you've made it easy for those who are hungry to learn more. Those who aren't will still benefit from hearing your key messages during the presentation. The worst thing you can do is post your final report on a website and expect that stakeholders will magically find their way towards it. Layering provides a trail for intended users to follow so they can dive deeper into the results if they choose.

I just put our long boring report on a buried web page in a format that requires it to be downloaded. Yet for some reason, nobody is reading it.

freshspectrum.com

To Handout or Not?

There's an ongoing debate in teaching and presentation circles as to whether or not you should distribute a handout during a presentation. The Yes side believes that audiences should have something to take notes on. The No side worries that instead of focusing on you and your message, attendees will pay more attention to the handout and read ahead on their own. I personally fall into the latter camp. When I'm giving a presentation, I want the audience's attention focused one hundred percent on what I'm saying. But I also understand the desire to have something concrete on which to take notes for later reference. Whatever you do, don't simply print out your slides. One solution is to inform your audience that you have a detailed handout, like a one-page brief, which you distribute at the end. You can even wave it around at the beginning to put their minds at ease. Another option is to use what's called a skeletal note, which is a customized handout with several key points and lots of blank space for participants to take notes. This satisfies the desire for a handout, but doesn't interfere with the focus on the presenter. Whichever way you choose, be sure to incorporate the principle of layering by including a URL on the handout where they can go for more detail if they desire.

Source: © 2006 Reprinted with permission from David Gray (www.xplaner.com) and Jeff Lash (www.jefflash.com).

One example of layering that I particularly like is from the US Government Accountability Office (GAO) below. For their 2017 *Improving Efficiency and Effectiveness* report, stakeholders had the option of reading a brief overview online, reading a more detailed background document, or downloading the full report. They also had the choice of listening to a podcast, viewing a short video, or downloading an infographic. If they were interested, stakeholders could also explore an Action Tracker data dashboard, where they could monitor the implementation of the report's recommendations.

This website is a great example of layering.

I'm guessing that by now some of you might be wondering how to condense your fifty-page report into a one-page handout. How is it possible to turn a whole burger into a sesame seed bun without losing all that taste and juiciness? Fortunately, there are two techniques that can help you significantly. The first is a method for distilling key messages from your content so they can be repeated throughout your layered communications (see *Your Key Messages* below). The second is a strategy for summarizing your content using index cards or sticky notes (see *Condensing Your Report* on page 30).

Your Key Messages

Thanks to Garr Reynolds' book, *Presentation Zen*,[15] I learned that one of the easiest ways to identify your key messages is to first close your computer or paper report. Then, using nothing but your own brain power, think about the three most important messages you want stakeholders to recall and/or do as a result of the evaluation. Ask yourself two questions:

- If they retained only one thought after attending your presentation, what should it be?
- If they did only one thing after reading your report, what should that be?

If you try it yourself, I'm sure you'll find these questions are usually not that hard to answer. I regularly get participants in my workshops to do it with ease.

Another technique that can help isolate your key messages is to ask yourself Five Whys about the evaluation.

1. Why are we conducting the evaluation?
   Because they want to know if the website is effective.

2. Why do they want to know if the website is effective?
   Because they need to know if visitors are using the information and resources.

3. Why do they want to know if visitors are using the information and resources?
   Because they need to know which methods are most effective for reaching this population.

4. Why do they need to know which methods are effective?
   So they can decide whether to maintain, expand, or discontinue the website.

5. Why do they need to know whether to maintain, expand, or discontinue?
   So they can appropriately budget for the next fiscal year.

Taken together, the answers to these Five Whys can help form the basis of one or more of your key messages.

As we'll see in Chapter 3, being able to summarize your report into two or three key messages is critical for making your findings stickier with stakeholders.

Condensing Your Report

Making your content suitable for layering requires serious cutting, and this can be a challenging task.

Here's another helpful trick I learned from Garr Reynolds.

1. Turn off your computer. (Yes!) This liberates your brain to think more creatively.

2. Write one of your key messages on an index card or sticky note. Repeat for all your key messages.

3. Begin to scribble additional highlights from your report onto separate cards and add them to make a storyboard.

4. Move the cards around until you've got a story with a logical flow. You might be surprised at the order you end up with!

5. Review your storyboard and add any other points you might have missed. If necessary, go back and look at the original report.

At this point, the cards in your storyboard might represent individual slides for a presentation, paragraphs of a newsletter, or perhaps sections of an infographic. If a card gives you an idea for a particular image that might represent that point, you can record that too. In this way, it's relatively easy to condense a large amount of information quickly.

This technique will also help you to develop an engaging flow to your content. When we think about summarizing a report, we tend to erroneously preserve the sections of the original report (Introduction, Methods, Results, Conclusion, and Recommendations) and pull tidbits from each.[16] But a slide presentation, fact sheet, or infographic is not a formal report, so use topical or informative headings instead to create an engaging storyline.

This is me in my kitchen condensing a report. I've pulled my initial key messages, and now I'm going through the report for any other items I might have missed. Each index card represents the subject of a presentation slide.

This is a nice 200 page comprehensive report.

Now can you cut it down to 2 pages? Maybe just take away the methods, evidence and findings.

freshspectrum

Layering can be a powerful technique in today's climate of shelved and forgotten final reports. By giving your stakeholders the choice to go as shallow or as deep as they choose into the results, you can ensure that at a minimum, some will hear your key messages. At the same time, others can find the greater detail and transparency they require.

Reorder Your Key Messages

As evaluators, most of us think and act like researchers. Unfortunately, we are also guilty of presenting like researchers because we've been trained to think and report inductively. We conscientiously lay out our data to build an argument, then formulate our conclusions and recommendations. But our end users are sometimes a different breed of animal. Managers are usually not scientists, so they tend to be concerned with issues such as finance or human resources. Their primary focus is on action, which is why they want to know what the recommendations and conclusions are first, before learning how you collected the data. When busy managers listen to your presentation, I

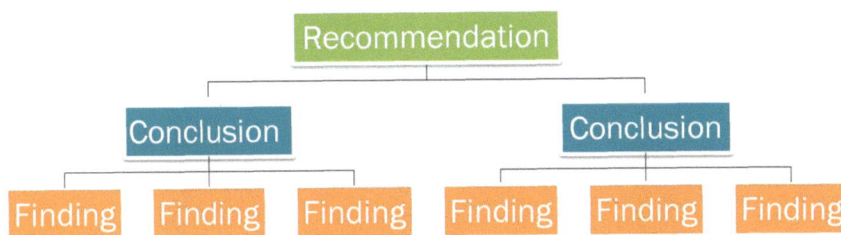

swear there's a little voice in the back of their minds that keeps saying, "Yes, I get it, but what should I do? Tell me what we need to do!" If you begin with your recommendations and conclusions, your audience or readers will know immediately where you are taking them. In my experience, the sooner you provide an "answer," the less impatient and more open they are to hearing how you actually derived it. This technique works for other audiences besides managers too.

I first learned about this technique from the business book, *The Pyramid Principle*, by Barbara Minto.[17] Journalists use it by starting every newspaper article off with a "lead." A lead is a sentence which summarizes the main points of the article followed by content of decreasing importance. Members of the military also employ it through use of the acronym B.L.U.F., which stands for Bottom Line Up Front. It works in an evaluation context as well.

Starting off a presentation with your recommendations may feel awkward at first, so here's a tip. Begin your talk by giving the audience a short overview of what you're going to cover in what order. For example,

> *Today I'm going to tell you about an evaluation of X, where we set out to answer the question, [your main evaluation question.] I'm going to begin by presenting our major conclusions and recommendations, and then explain how we came to these.*

Reordering your key messages is an easy way to grab the attention of busy managers and better influence their use of the results.

The Shark Tank

An evaluator I know (I'll call him Bob) works in a large organization conducting complex and lengthy evaluations. When Bob finishes an evaluation, he is required to present his findings to the organization's senior executive team. Usually, he is given thirty minutes or so to do this, but what often happens is the meeting gets behind schedule and his time is shortened. As he's waiting outside the board room (he calls it "the shark tank") for his turn, it's not unusual for his thirty minutes to get whittled down to ten or even five minutes. Over the years, Bob has accepted that he won't always get his thirty minutes to present. Sometimes it's five minutes or nothing. Imagine, five minutes to present the results of a two-year evaluation! But this is sometimes a reality in today's fast-paced world. In this situation, it's wise to start at the top of the pyramid with the answer, i.e., your evaluation conclusions and recommendations, and then explain how you got there, time permitting.

In fact, if I was ever in this situation, I'd simply tell a sticky story (see *Stories* on page 41).

You now have four principles to guide your reporting. If you're able to: Target Your Audience; Develop a Communications Plan; Layer Your Content; and Reorder Your Key Messages; you'll be pleasantly surprised how much the effectiveness of your evaluation reporting improves.

But what about the content of your reports? In the next chapter, we'll look at ways you can make this content more engaging and sticky.

Chapter Summary

- Four principles for more effective reporting are: Target Your Audience; Develop a Communications Plan; Layer Your Content; and Reorder Your Key Messages.

- Different stakeholder groups have diverse information needs from an evaluation. Distinguish the various target audiences for your report in order to tailor the content and style of the communication to their specific concerns.

- Draft a formal communication plan to identify the most appropriate types of report for each of your different audiences, and assign an appropriate timeframe, budget, and priority.

- Layering is the simultaneous use of different, but linked, report formats to communicate evaluation results. Layering allows stakeholders to go as shallow or as deep as they choose into the evaluation findings.

- Reorder your key messages and begin with the recommendations and conclusions to better engage the attention of busy managers.

Chapter 3 - What Makes Your Content Sticky?

From an evaluation perspective, sticky means your stakeholders can understand, recall, and act on key findings, conclusions, and recommendations. The concept of stickiness originally came from Malcolm Gladwell's popular book, *The Tipping Point*.[18] In their 2007 bestseller *Made to Stick*,[19] Chip and Dan Heath illustrate in further detail what's necessary to make messages sticky. *Made to Stick* is probably one of the most useful non-evaluation books I've ever read for my evaluation practice. In this chapter, I've summarized the book's key points that are most relevant for effective reporting.

The Curse of Knowledge

To fully appreciate stickiness, it's necessary to first understand the *Curse of Knowledge*.[20] Most evaluators I know, including myself, suffer from this affliction. By the time we've spent months or even years on an evaluation, we've developed such an in-depth knowledge and familiarity with the results it's hard for us to imagine what it's like to be a stakeholder hearing the results for the first time. We can't un-know what we intimately know about the data. Traditionally we have circumvented the Curse of Knowledge by pouring everything we know into long final reports, but this can overwhelm our intended users and discourage utilization. Because the Curse of Knowledge affects our capacity to communicate succinctly, it also hampers our ability to develop key messages that are sticky. But don't feel bad, because communications courses are not a standard part of most evaluation training. Thankfully, however, there is something we can do to break the curse.

Stickiness

The authors of *Made to Stick* argue that sticky messages have six things in common:

- Simplicity
- Unexpectedness
- Concreteness
- Credibility
- Emotions
- Stories

LEARNING OBJECTIVE

After reading this chapter, you will be able to:

- List six elements of sticky communication.

They use the mnemonic, SUCCESs, to help readers remember them. Let's look at each briefly.

Simplicity

Sticky messages have been stripped down and simplified to their bare essentials.

Determine what your absolute core messages are, i.e., what you wish your stakeholders to recall and act on, and write them succinctly in one sentence (see *Your Key Messages* on page 29). Your goal here is not to dumb down your main findings, but rather reduce the noise surrounding them. The more noise you reduce, the more evident and stickier your key messages will be.

Evaluators are always worried about oversimplifying when communicating their results. One way to avoid this is to incorporate flags into your key messages. Flags are things that cue readers into their own pre-existing mental models: beliefs, ideas, and images that are consciously or unconsciously formed from personal experience. Flags allow you to efficiently communicate more complex concepts using simple phrases because they tie into ideas the reader is already familiar with. Analogies and proverbs are good examples of flags.

A well-thought-out simple idea can be amazingly powerful in shaping behaviour.

Chip and Dan Heath
Made to Stick

Keep the Baby

I once evaluated an older program on behalf of a funder. The funder believed the program had serious problems and was either going to cost a lot of money to fix or need to be terminated. It turns out it was still on track and only required minor tweaks. I wanted to make a recommendation that most of the program was worth saving, so I adapted the mental flag, "Don't throw the baby out with the bathwater," in my presentation to the board. The phrase, "Keep the baby," ended up being far more powerful than, "The effective aspects of the program should be maintained in their current state." (And darn cuter too.) I know this because staff continued to refer to this phrase in meetings and communications with me for several months afterwards.

Unexpectedness

To make your findings stick in the minds of decision makers, you need to first grab their attention. One way to do this is present something unexpected in your key messages. The element of surprise makes us wake up and pay attention, and fixes content more powerfully into our memories. For example, many people recall where they were when they heard that John F. Kennedy, Princess Diana, or Michael Jackson died. I typically think of unexpected ideas as the interesting tidbits I remember to share with my family over dinner.

Review your findings for any unexpected implications. For example, in the *Keep the Baby* example, the funder anticipated they would have to terminate or spend a lot of money revamping the program. Instead, the evaluation indicated the program was actually *saving* them money.

One way to incorporate unexpectedness is to create a mystery to be solved. *Made to Stick* calls this a *knowledge gap* or *curiosity gap* because it hints at what stakeholders don't yet know. As evaluators, we typically give our intended users a lot of facts (our findings), but first we need to make them realize they actually need this information. Engage your stakeholders by taking them on a journey where the ending is unknown. They'll be more disposed to stick around for the answer. For example, you might say,

> *In this evaluation, we set out to answer the question, 'How worthwhile are the outcomes from this program and why do stakeholders feel so strongly about it?'*

Because of the Curse of Knowledge, you may need to run your findings by someone not intimately involved in the evaluation to determine whether there is anything unexpected in the results. A data party is a great way to accomplish this (see *Data Parties* in Chapter 2).

Love Your Street Nurse

Remember the Syphilis Blitz I evaluated in Chapter 2? Every street nurse I interviewed told me unequivocally how much they and their clients hated being involved in the intervention. But after dozens of interviews and focus groups with their clients, it was clear the clients actually *loved* the street nurses even more as a result of the initiative. When it came time to present, I led with this point in my presentation and had them hooked for the rest of the two-hour session.

Concreteness

The more concrete a concept, the stickier it becomes because it often prompts a visual cue in the mind of those receiving the message. When people ask me what I do for a living, I usually try not to explain what an evaluator does. Instead, I give them one or two examples of evaluations I'm currently working on.

Review your key messages for abstract concepts and replace them with more concrete examples. Your goal here is to avoid the dry business language that plagues many evaluation reports. Again, if you can take advantage of flags or concepts that people are already familiar with, they will be even more powerful. For example, you can replace the vague statement, "increased capacity-building," with something more tangible such as "monthly lunch and learn sessions" or "mentoring." As evaluators, we're highly skilled at making the abstract more concrete so we can measure it, but we have a tendency to slip back into the abstract when we report our results.

One way to make your evaluation findings more concrete is to present them from the perspective of a particular entity, such as a participant or community, and describe specifically how the program has impacted them. These stories or testimonials not only bring your findings to life, they add a small dose of credibility as well.

Concreteness makes your findings more clear so intended users can act on them. When my daughter was in kindergarten, I used to get frustrated because nothing would happen when I asked her to clean up her room. Then I realized she needed more concrete direction, such as "Put the crayons in the box. Stack the books on the shelf. Put your shirt in the laundry hamper." It's the same with evaluation recommendations. When I'm writing recommendations, I try to imagine the current program manager is replaced by a new one who knows nothing about the evaluation. The more specific and concrete the recommendations, the easier the new person can pick up the ball and get things rolling. (See *Recommendations That Rock* in the Appendix.)

Sometimes it feels uncomfortable to reduce our extensive evaluation findings to one or two concrete examples because of the dreaded Curse of Knowledge. There's so much more to include! But thanks to the principle of layering, you can relax a little knowing that you have options to expand your messages beyond one single type of report.

> **As evaluators, we're highly skilled at making the abstract more concrete so we can measure it. But we have a tendency to slip back into the abstract when we report our results.**

Splash and Ripple

In my evaluation workshops, I often use PLAN:NET's excellent Splash and Ripple analogy to explain logic models.[21] A rock denotes the inputs, dropping the rock symbolizes the activities, the splash that occurs represents the outputs, and the resulting ripples are the short, intermediate, and long-term outcomes. Time and time again I see the light bulbs go on above people's heads when I drop a small rock into my daughter's Barbie pool filled with water at the front of the room. I can think of no better way to make an abstract concept like a logic model more concrete for learners.

Credibility

Credibility also plays a role in making concepts sticky. As evaluators, we tend to establish credibility through the use of evaluation methodology or statistics. But if we're concerned with stickiness, credibility becomes something entirely different.

The authors of *Made to Stick* note that the most obvious sources of credibility, external validation and statistics, aren't always the stickiest. Instead, they recommend incorporating vivid details into your key messages rather than presenting users with an overwhelming torrent of statistics. Vivid details are ones that reinforce the core idea but also make it noteworthy and memorable.

Whenever it's my turn to tell a ghost story around the campfire, I always revert to one I remember hearing when I was 10 years old. You might even know it; the one where the boyfriend's shoes are making scratching sounds on the top of the car. Ghost stories are essentially urban legends, which are the Krazy Glue of stickiness. The reason I remember this story is not only because it scared the bejeezus out of me (see *Emotions* on page 40), but also because it was told exceptionally well by my friend's older brother, who didn't hold back on the vivid, and highly gory, details.

If you employ the principle of layering, you can still create a link to the statistics in a long report or appendix, should a reader be interested in them. If you must quote statistics in your key messages, place them into a more concrete context that better illustrates what the statistics represent. For example, if 60% of participants in a program experience a particular positive outcome, you could ask policy makers to imagine what it would be like if the program was scaled up to affect six out of every ten individuals in a larger population of need.

> **The most obvious sources of credibility—external validation and statistics—aren't always the stickiest.**
>
> Chip and Dan Heath
> *Made to Stick*

Sticky Statistics?

Several years ago, I volunteered for a social enterprise that developed educational software for primary students in Africa. Over time the evaluation determined that mean reading scores were a whopping 25 percent higher for students who used the software versus those that didn't. Years later I couldn't recall this exact figure, so I went back to my files and looked it up. But one thing I have always remembered from the evaluation is a Grade 2 teacher in the intervention group who said, "I've never had a Grade 2 class who can read before."

Including stories or interview quotes from program recipients or ambassadors is another way to foster credibility. Imagine the impact of you, the evaluator, describing the results of a literacy evaluation as opposed to a participant who has just successfully learned to read in the program.

Vivid Details

I once evaluated a peer educator project where I was able to use vivid details to increase the credibility of my message. For two years, the BCCDC Outreach Street Nurse Program used paid peer educators to enhance their HIV prevention and education work on the street. Once funds for the project ended, the peer educators no longer received an honorarium for their work. However, I was struck by the number who showed up for an evaluation interview still carrying their "Peer Educator" labelled shoulder bag filled with health education supplies, seven months after the program had ended. I wanted to make a point about the ongoing sustainability of using peer volunteers in this capacity so I verbally painted a detailed picture for managers of these individuals still carrying their bags around daily.

Emotions

One way to craft more memorable messages and spur people to action is to make stakeholders truly *care* about an issue, which requires the use of emotion.

The authors of *Made to Stick* note that when we are thinking analytically, we are less likely to think emotionally. Look for opportunities to link your key messages with an emotion. You don't have to reduce a meeting room full of policy makers to tears, but consider telling a story or fact that arouses some form of emotional response such as surprise, apprehension, anticipation, or pride.

Emotions drive action because they motivate people to care. Nonprofit fundraisers have understood this concept for years. They build empathy into their appeals because they know that people are more likely to donate to an issue such as an orphaned child or an abandoned animal rather than an abstract statement regarding rates of HIV or animal cruelty.

Your first task in making stakeholders care is to link something they don't currently care about (your findings) to something they do. Like the earlier use of flags, you will find it easier to elicit emotions from intended users if you can associate your results with mental models, flags, or stimuli that universally make us feel laughter, excitement, or grief for example. I'm not advocating that we put cute puppies on the cover of our evaluation reports, but look for examples, stories, and images that will evoke some form of emotional response.

Are we making a difference?

This slide evokes an emotional response.

REFLECT

What about you? Think about a strong memory you have. Are there any emotions associated with it? How can you make this happen with your audience as well?

One of the easiest ways to use emotion for greater stickiness is to appeal to stakeholder self-interest. Addressing the question, "What's in it for me?", in your communications can be effective, but don't be afraid to also appeal to people's higher order values of caring and identity, such as community, justice, fairness, and equality.

Stories

Stories are the glue that brings all the other elements of stickiness together. They usually have a single point, contain unexpected surprises, use concrete language, are based on credible, real-life scenarios, and evoke some sort of emotion. They're also a heck of a lot more entertaining than the average executive summary.

In evaluation, we often present our findings as a slow-reveal argument intended to persuade an audience to act (see *Reorder Your Key Messages* on page 31). Stories, however, are more efficient, engaging, and inspiring while at the same time instructional. In academic-speak, they're called case studies or narratives.

The most obvious use of stories in evaluation reporting is to ask participants to share a story of how a program has impacted them. You can also use stories to counter skepticism in managers by illustrating the implications of proposed recommendations and action steps. In my first book, I incorporated multiple stories about organizations successfully dealing with program sustainability to illustrate my key points.

Stories in Reports

Everybody loves a good story, even high-powered policy makers. Case studies, Most Significant Change* stories, and other forms of narrative are valuable for bringing macro level outcomes down to a personal level to better engage readers. I prefer to use the term "story" instead of "narrative" because it reminds us to actually tell a story. Your story doesn't need to be long and sophisticated; a few paragraphs will do. If you populate it with real-life characters and situations, policy-makers will remember it long after they've read your report.

A story about a program participant fits nicely as a sidebar in a two-pager or a traditional-style report.[22]

SUCCESs for Stickiness

Mnemonics are another technique for increasing information retention, so use the SUCCESs prompt (Simple, Unexpected, Concrete, Credible, Emotions, and Stories) to help you craft more powerful key messages. You can start slowly and build your confidence by focusing on only one or two elements to start. Once you begin, you'll find it easier to integrate them more regularly into your practice.

Most of the examples in *Made to Stick* focus on written or verbal communications. But as you'll see next, visuals can also significantly increase our ability to understand and recall information.

Visual Stickiness

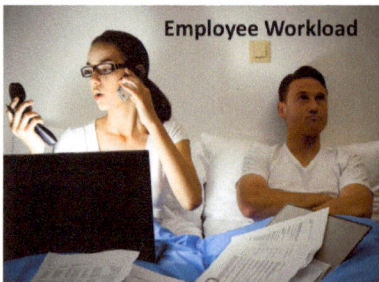

Text is more powerful when paired with a visual.

In the book, *Brain Rules*,[23] John Medina explains how vision is the most dominant of all our senses. As he says, "Professionals everywhere need to know about the incredible inefficiency of text-based information and the incredible effects of images." Researchers are still determining to what extent visuals, or visuals paired with text, excel at promoting recall,[24, 25, 26] but we're beginning to understand that our brains are more efficient at interpreting pictures than text. [27, 28, 29]

* For more information on the Most Significant Change approach visit http://www.betterevaluation.org/en/plan/approach/most_significant_change.

Barbra Streisand was a Neuroscientist

"Memories, like the corners of my mind…"

If you recognize this line from the song, "The Way We Were," by Barbra Streisand, you might be like me and have a mental model of a seventies hit now played in lonely airport lounges. But when it comes to appreciating the role of visuals in enhancing stickiness, it's necessary to understand our different forms of memory. In her book, *Presenting Data Effectively,*[30] Stephanie Evergreen explains the role of visual dominance, also known as the "pictorial superiority effect," in enhancing what we remember.

If we want policy makers to recall our findings and recommendations in three months' time, the information from our report has to move through three phases of memory: early attention, working memory, and long-term memory. Early attention is the phase where information merely catches our eye. Working memory uses a bit more brain power to process the information for activities like reasoning, decision-making, and behavior. Long-term memory is what stores the information for recall and possible use later.

We can use the Pictorial Superiority Effect to our advantage by choosing engaging and relevant visuals to grab the early attention of stakeholders. Once we have their attention, working memory kicks in and begins to process what they're seeing. Working memory is like the brain's own computer RAM. It can only process and store limited amounts of information for short periods of time, but while the information is there it's actively being used. If you overload your working memory, it's like getting a spinning cursor on your computer (a.k.a. the Wheel of Death). The system just can't handle it.

It's the same with our brains. If you overload your audience with results, less information will be stored in their long-term memory. Despite what Barbra Streisand says, your findings will not make it to the corners of their mind. Research tells us that most people can retain about four pieces of information in their working memory at any one time.[31, 32] Visuals reduce the overload on working memory, thus increasing the chances that more information will successfully move to long-term memory. Visuals are also an easy way to incorporate the use of flags in key messages because they activate our pre-existing mental models.

When recall is important, aim to enhance your text as much as possible with visuals.

Professionals everywhere need to know about the incredible inefficiency of text-based information and the incredible effects of images.

John Medina
Brain Rules

Putting it All Together

If you pair visuals with the SUCCESs concepts I discussed earlier (Simplicity, Unexpectedness, Concreteness, Credibility, Emotions, and Stories), you'll have an effective strategy for promoting the recall of your evaluation's key messages, which in turn is an excellent way to foster greater utilization.

Now you're armed with tips on how to make your findings stickier. However, but you may still be stuck having to use a long report. Let's begin to look at ways to improve the format of your traditional evaluation reports.

Chapter Summary

- Sticky findings are ones your stakeholders can understand, recall, and act on later.

- Your key messages are more likely to be sticky if they follow Chip and Dan Heath's SUCCESs formula; they are simple, unexpected, concrete, credible, elicit emotion, and tell a story.

- Simple messages have been reduced to their most important essentials to decrease surrounding noise. If stakeholders do only one thing after reading your report, what should it be?

- To grab the early attention of stakeholders, present something unexpected from your findings and create a sense of mystery that hints at what stakeholders don't yet know.

- Use visual cues and replace abstract concepts with more tangible examples to make your messages more concrete.

- Increase credibility by incorporating vivid details that reinforce the core idea of a key message rather than overwhelming stakeholders with statistics.

- Look for opportunities to link your key messages with an emotion in order to inspire stakeholders to care and spur them to action.

- Stories are the glue that brings all the other elements of stickiness together. They have a simple message, contain unexpected surprises, use concrete language, are based on credible scenarios, and usually evoke some sort of emotion.

- Incorporate visuals as much as possible with text to decrease the load placed on working memory to enhance recall.

Chapter 4 - Common Report Errors

Whenever I give a workshop on innovative reporting, there is always at least one participant who feels unable to abandon the traditional final report format. I get it. These folks usually work for a large institution (often government or academia), or have a funder that demands a long report. Or, they're concerned that if they don't present the entire works, the report won't be transparent enough. Other evaluators who work with smaller community organizations tell me they're sometimes asked for a long and thorough report because it appears more credible and makes it easier to justify the evaluation to the funders. If this is your situation, take heart. While some of us are able to freely experiment with alternatives, others simply can't. Before we look at innovative alternatives, let's turn our attention to the standard final report and what we can do to make it friendlier.

Here are seven issues that I find particularly annoying about long reports and simple ways to deal with them.

Executive Summary is Too Long

The executive summary plays a key role in the traditional-style report as it is often what entices or discourages a reader from diving in further. The ideal executive summary is two pages, but sometimes it's a struggle to stay within those limits. There may simply be too much content for two measly pages. Other times the problem is verbal diarrhea.

I would rather people read an attractively-designed four-page executive summary than nothing at all. But where is it written that an executive summary must be text only? One day I joined an American Evaluation Association Coffee Break webinar where Nate Wilairat presented an innovative idea for incorporating data dashboard items into executive summaries like the example on the following page. It's amazing how the addition of a dashboard, chart, image, or my personal favorite, a matrix, can make a document more engaging yet still convey critical information in only two pages.

LEARNING OBJECTIVE

After reading this chapter, you will be able to:

• List common report errors and ways to address them.

REFLECT

Take a moment to think about everything that bothers you about the standard final report. What makes it less engaging or less sticky for stakeholders? What is it about the long report that impedes use?

These executive summaries by Nate Wilairat and EMI Consulting incorporate dashboard metrics and matrices to make the content more engaging.[33]

Too Much Jargon

The perils of too much jargon in evaluation reports are well-known. Sometimes it's appropriate for your target group, but more often than not it isn't. Jargon is sneaky, and it can often slip in without us knowing it. One way to jargon proof a document is to give it to a colleague in another field who can spot these instances immediately.

Key Findings Are Hard to Find

Jane Davidson, an evaluator based in New Zealand and the US, once wrote an enlightened editorial in the *Journal of Multidisciplinary Evaluation* titled, "Unlearning Some of Our Social Science Habits."[34] In it, she questions why our evaluation reports always seem to take the form of an academic journal article with the following headings: Introduction, Methods, Results, Discussion, Conclusions, and Recommendations. While this structure might make sense for a Masters thesis, it certainly doesn't work for the busy manager who needs information fast. Imagine a policy maker, prepping for an important meeting. How will they find the answer to their question quickly when it is buried in a section simply called Results? Jane recommends that we organize our findings using the evaluation questions as topical headers. Using topical headers helps readers to scan the Table of Contents and find what they need immediately. While I admit there's probably still a role for the traditional headers such as Introduction, Methods, and Results in many reports, we can make them a lot more accessible to readers if we at least use our evaluation questions as sub-headers in the Results section.

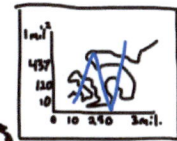

I doubt if anyone could find the information they need in this example I came across, let alone a busy decision maker.

Topical themes dramatically increase the reader's ability to predict content and read more like a story.

Nancy Duarte
Slidedocs: Spread Ideas with Effective Visual Documents

Reporting Too Much Data

Years ago, I conducted a needs assessment of HIV organizations in the province of British Columbia. I wanted to find out what barriers prevented these agencies from doing more outcome evaluation. During one of the interviews, a program staff person said to me, "Sometimes it seems like we're collecting data just for collection's sake." The same week, the program's funder told me, "They send me all this data in their reports, and I don't know what to do with it."

This is absurd, I thought.

The same problem affects our evaluation reports. Because of the Curse of Knowledge, we tend to cram them full of data, thinking it will make our argument stronger. But sometimes all this does is overwhelm the reader. The more data we collect, the more compelled we feel to report it. Worse still is the tendency to include large amounts of quantitative data. You know, the hard, crunchy kind. Michael Quinn Patton once said, "My experience with stakeholders suggests that they would rather have soft data about an important question than hard data about an issue of less relevance."[35] Einstein also reportedly said something similar, "Everything that can be counted does not necessarily count; everything that counts cannot necessarily be counted." I think this is often true with evaluation reports. Don't get me wrong, I'm not necessarily saying we should cut down on our data collection (although I do think there are times where it wouldn't hurt), but the principle of layering applies well here. If you are able to move some information to the appendices to make a report more appealing to a reader, do so.

Missing Windows of Opportunity

As evaluators, we pride ourselves on using the most rigorous methodology possible, but sometimes we get so caught up in our evaluation plan or waiting for anticipated data that we miss windows of opportunity where decision makers can use our evidence. I'm guilty myself of sometimes focusing on my own evaluation timeline versus the planning and budget cycles of the organizations I work with. In many cases, managers will not or cannot wait for our final report before making a decision. This is because they have other inputs to consider such as budgetary and political factors, or organizational protocols.

In my experience, many managers still haven't made the connection between evaluation and decision-making. It is our job as evaluators to determine upfront how and when managers plan to use our findings and then work to meet *their* deadlines, not ours. Timing evaluation reports effectively may require you to release interim findings before the evaluation is complete. This is fine as long as you include a discussion of the limitations or uncertainty associated with these early results. While this practice may make some uncomfortable, consider the benefits of a comprehensive report versus missed opportunities for actual use.

Too Much Narrative

Final reports that are nothing but narrative are a pet peeve of mine. When I see pages and pages of text like the example below, my brain tends to go into sleep mode.

> Blah blah blah blah blah blah blah blah blah blah blah blah blah blah blah blah blah blah blah blah blah blah blah blah blah. Something really important here that the reader might miss. blah blah blah blah blah blah blah blah blah blah blah blah blah blah blah blah blah blah blah blah blah blah blah blah blah blah blah blah blah blah.

I worry about how much important content is missed by readers when it's buried in paragraph after paragraph of text. As we learned in Chapter 3, pairing text with visuals is more engaging and effective. It's trite to say, but a picture is still worth a thousand words when it comes to evaluation reports. Luckily, we can easily fix this problem by breaking up the text with lots of headings and sub-headings, lists, icons, images, charts, pull-quotes, dashboards, and matrices.

Ignoring Report Design

In 2010, Stephanie Evergreen finished her dissertation on how evaluators and researchers present their data. Two books and hundreds of keynotes and workshops later, she has significantly changed the way evaluators approach data visualization and report formatting.[36] Thanks to her work we better understand how the layout of a chart or page in an evaluation report can positively or negatively influence how effectively that information is registered and stored in the minds of readers. Many in the field of evaluation have embraced these new practices and continue to push the standards for report design to new levels of effectiveness. While Stephanie's work is too detailed to summarize here, I urge you to spend some time learning more about how the various elements of report design contribute to greater utilization.

Report Format Checklist

I'm always preaching about shorter reports, but I do understand there are situations where a long report is required. If this is your situation, The Evaluation Centre at Western Michigan University has developed a *Checklist for Program Evaluation Report Content*, which they've allowed me to reprint for you in the Appendix.

Although you still might be stuck having to prepare lengthy reports, there are simple things you can do to make them more digestible and engaging for your readers. Keep in mind that expectations for a long report don't preclude you from employing the principle of layering and using other innovative forms of reporting at the same time. In the next chapter, we'll look at some alternatives you may wish to try.

I'm not a
visual person.

How about
your audience?

freshspectrum.com

Chapter Summary

- Not everyone can abandon the long report, but there are techniques to make it more engaging.

- Dashboards, charts, icons, images, and matrices are easy ways to make a two-page executive summary more engaging.

- Use topical themes, such as the evaluation questions, as headers and sub-headers to make it easier for stakeholders to locate specific information in the report.

- Avoid burying key content in pages and pages of narrative. Break up long sections of text with headings and sub-headings, paragraphs, lists, icons, images, charts, pull-quotes, and matrices.

- Move extraneous data to the appendices to make the report less overwhelming to read.

- Time the release of reports to coincide with stakeholders' own timelines for decision-making.

- Attention to data visualization and the layout of pages in an evaluation report can positively influence recall and utilization.

Chapter 5 - Alternatives to a Final Report

When I first started exploring evaluation reporting in 2008, I had no idea of the extent to which this area would explode. Evaluators have now wholeheartedly embraced new ways of communicating their findings. Some days it's all I can do to keep up with the new ideas emerging. In this chapter, I briefly describe several of the most promising innovations to date. My intent is to inspire you to think beyond the long report and experiment with something new. While some of you will be able to use these ideas in place of your regular reports, others will opt to use one or more of them in addition to it, as part of a layering strategy. You'll also likely find that some formats work well for certain audiences, but not for others.

LEARNING OBJECTIVE

After reading this chapter, you will be able to:

• State innovative alternatives to the traditional-style report.

Dr. McCoy Moments

If you've ever watched reruns of the original Star Trek, you'll know that whenever the medical officer, Dr. McCoy, feels under pressure he'll say, "I'm a doctor Spock, not a mechanic!" As evaluators everywhere continue to raise the bar in innovative reporting, I confess to having my own share of Dr. McCoy moments. Sometimes I find myself trying to design communication materials that are way beyond my skill set. "I'm an evaluator, not a graphic designer!" I also don't have the evaluation budget to hire professional designers for help. Thankfully, this isn't always necessary. In this chapter, I highlight some low-tech options you can use with similar results.

Presentations

Oral presentations

Oral presentations, with or without slides, are one of the most common forms of evaluation reporting. Unfortunately, they don't receive nearly the attention they should which is why I've put them first. Everyone is so focused on slide design these days, but public speaking is an important soft skill that evaluators also need in their toolbox. If stakeholders don't read our full reports, we at least hope they will listen to us talk for a few minutes. But if our oral presentations are dull, we risk losing a critical dissemination opportunity. Put another way, if our audience doesn't like the sesame seed bun, they're certainly not going to eat the lettuce, tomato, cheese, or patty.

Several years ago, I sat at the back of a conference presentation feeling incredibly bored and frustrated because I knew that excellent content was being lost due to lacklustre delivery. To help pass the time, I crafted a list of 22 do's and don'ts for presentations on the next page.

22 Tips for Better Presentations

If public speaking terrifies you, here are 22 practical tips that will kick-start your presentation skills. Soon you'll be managing your jitters, engaging your audience, and zooming through your presentations like a pro.

Speak to Engage

1. **Blah, Blah, Blah.** Avoid reading from a prepared speech, or reading directly from your slides.

2. **Increase Interaction.** Seek to engage your audience through greater interaction. Adult learners often appreciate much of what you are saying, they just need to be reminded of it. If you acknowledge your audience for their own experience, their level of involvement will increase significantly. Interactive techniques can range from something simple, like asking questions, taking an informal poll, or giving people a short quiz to do in their seats, to more complex activities such as putting them in small groups and assigning them a simple task.

3. **Get Personal.** Wherever possible, weave your own personal stories and examples into your talk. Storytelling can help you relax on stage, and it immediately brings people's attention back into the room.

4. **Use Novelty.** Don't discount the power of using unexpected novelty in your presentation. I still remember dozing off in a talk when the presenter suddenly put on a large Dr. Seuss hat. Bing! I was suddenly wide-awake.

5. **Deal with Monopolizers.** If you have an audience member who is monopolizing the discussion, you can do three things:

   - Paraphrase what they've said, so they feel heard.

   - Slowly and subtly walk towards them decreasing the size of their 'stage.'

   - Say, "Thank you for that, let's see what someone else has to say."

Move Around

6. **Get Moving.** Try to get out from behind the lectern or table and move around the room as much as possible.

7. **Use a Wireless Presenter.** Using a wireless presenter will give you more freedom to move around the room and make you look like a pro.

8. **Be Aware of Your Screen.** Avoid walking in front of the projector screen as it's very distracting for your audience. If necessary, use masking tape to map out a safe zone on the carpet.

Practice

9. **Practice Your Presentation Beforehand.** Most of us know this, but very few of us do it! I'm not sure why. Perhaps because we all secretly love to live dangerously. However, the peace of mind and confidence that comes from being prepared will convince the audience of your sincerity.

10. **Get Feedback from a Trusted Source.** Without realizing it, you may be gesturing or speaking in a distracting or unnecessary way. Get a second opinion from someone you trust who will be honest with you.

11. **Get Professional Help.** If you haven't been to a Toastmasters meeting, you'll be surprised at how useful they are. The meetings are fun, the people are supportive, and chances are there is a lunchtime meeting close to where you work. (See *Nervous About Public Speaking* on page 54?)

Timing

12. **Time it Right.** Avoid frustrating your audience by taking 80% of your allotted time to cover 20% of your presentation and then rush through the last five minutes. Most of us speak slower than we read, so if you've followed Tip #9, your timing will be bang on.

13. **Warn Me.** If you're not able to speak and watch the clock at the same time, ask a co-presenter or colleague to give you subtle ten, five, and two-minute warnings.

The Title

14. **Choose Your Session Title Wisely.** Think like your audience. What will they expect from the title of your talk? If it doesn't accurately convey the topic of your presentation, you will have dissatisfied people leaving halfway through, which is distracting for everyone.

15. **Keep Your Title Broad.** If you have points of interest for a broad audience, avoid including too many specifics in your title so potential attendees won't discount your presentation as something outside their area of interest.

Slides

16. **Fix Your Slides.** Badly formatted slides can kill your presentation. Educate yourself on the new best practices in slide design. (See *Slides* on page 54.)

17. **Take a Test Drive.** Arrive in plenty of time to thoroughly test your equipment and get comfortable with it.

Structure

18. **Use Learning Objectives.** Open and close your presentation with clear learning objectives, even if it's only twenty minutes. Correctly written learning objectives are statements of what participants will be able to do at the end of the session, e.g., "At the end of this session you will be able to state four best practices for designing slides." Note that "to understand" is not a learning objective. Use action verbs like "list," "describe," "distinguish," and "explain" instead.

19. **Close the Loop.** Repeat your learning objectives at the end of your presentation to help integrate learning.

20. **Three Key Messages.** Decide what are your three key points and repeat them several times during your presentation.

Handouts

21. **Offer Takeaways.** Provide take-aways in the form of handouts, tools, and other items that give your audience the impression of value for their time spent.

22. **Make Enough Copies.** If you're going to distribute a hard copy handout, make sure you have sufficient copies. This will prevent distractions and scuffles in the audience for scarce copies.

A successful presentation is all about leaving your audience feeling informed and satisfied. If you speak to engage, move around, practice, time it right, improve your slides, and reinforce your key messages, you will be a better presenter instantly.

Nervous About Public Speaking?

Presentations are a common aspect of evaluation reporting. However, if it's true that people fear public speaking more than death, I'm surprised at how few evaluators are aware of *Toastmasters International*. Originally formed in 1905, today's Toastmasters is not the men's club that your father used to attend. I went to my first Toastmasters meeting in my early twenties and was surprised to be officially greeted at the door by another young woman dressed in goth style (jet black hair, black leather, loads of black eyeliner, and multiple body piercings). I was even more surprised when she rose at the beginning of the meeting to formally introduce me in a manner that rivalled any speech Hillary Clinton could make. *Holy smokes*, I thought, *if Toastmasters can help me speak like that, I'm sold.* I've been attending Toastmaster meetings on and off throughout my professional career and I can't think of a safer or more enjoyable atmosphere to practice the art of public speaking. Best of all, there's usually a friendly Toastmasters group near you. Visit http://www.toastmasters.org.

Oral presentations are a powerful form of communication for evaluators, but getting key people to attend your presentation in today's busy workplace can be a struggle. Here are a few strategies to increase participation:

- Ask to be included on the agenda of a regularly scheduled meeting instead of expecting everyone to convene a meeting around you.

- Offer to bring food. Yummy food. A sandwich tray just doesn't cut it anymore.

- Incorporate interactive elements into your presentation to make it more engaging. Inform attendees ahead of time that you will require their input on several critical issues.

- Consider holding an interactive data party instead. We now recognize data parties as an important step in the evaluation process for engaging stakeholders and increasing use.

- If possible, recruit program recipients to help you present. Putting a human face to your findings will make them exceedingly sticky.

Slides

If you haven't already noticed, there has been a revolution in slide design over the past decade. Today's slide presentations are not the snooze fest they used to be. Greater use of images and design principles have created more captivating slides and as a result, happier, more alert audiences. I'm thrilled with the progress our profession as a whole has made in raising the bar for more engaging presentations. Thanks to authors like Garr Reynolds, Nancy Duarte, and Edward Tufte, plus the American Evaluation Association's *Potent Presentations Initiative* and the Data Visualization Topical Interest Group's annual conference slide clinic, the quality of presentation slides at conferences has increased phenomenally over the years.

Excellent slides are characterized by:

- six or fewer words
- minimum 30 pt. font
- sans serif font
- dark text on a light background
- no bullets
- left-aligned text and headers
- high-quality images, e.g., not blurry or stretched disproportionately
- images that are related to the content
- images that touch the edge of the slide (full-bleed)
- clutter-free backgrounds with lots of empty white space
- logos on the first and last slides only
- minimal animation or fancy transitions
- one idea per slide.[37]

Why all these changes? Savvy presenters can again thank the Pictorial Superiority Effect, which tells us that people recall images better than just text. Savvy presenters design their slide shows to tell a story about the evaluation rather than follow the traditional heading structure of an academic journal article. They choose photos that are directly relevant to their topic and ideally elicit some form of emotion to make them stickier. They avoid cheesy stock photos of good-looking professionals shaking hands and over-used clipart of skinny alien men and puzzle pieces. When they download stock photos, they select an ideal size of 1280 by 720 pixels. If they work for an institution that forces them to brand each slide, they do so sparingly and as small as possible to avoid taking away from the content of the slide. They eschew pre-baked slide templates in favour of a simple white background. They put the most important information in the top left quadrant.

Savvy presenters also do not read directly from their slides because they realize that a slide deck is not a script. Remember how the average person reads at a rate of 300 words per minute (or higher)? Most people speak at a rate of only 150 words per minute.[38] Therefore, if you simply read your bullet points to the audience, they will have read to the bottom of the screen and be bored in no time flat. Death by Power Point indeed.

Pinterest

For a comprehensive listing of resources for this chapter, check out my Pinterest page, *Effective Evaluation Reporting*, with over 200 ideas, tools, and techniques for better evaluation reporting. (https://www.pinterest.com/evaluationmaven/evaluation-reporting/)

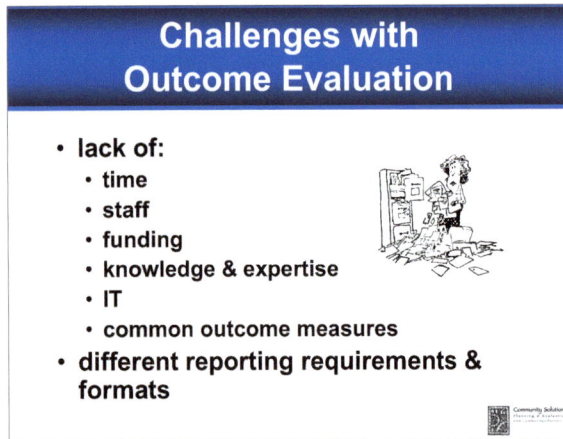

This is a slide I made before I learned about slide design.

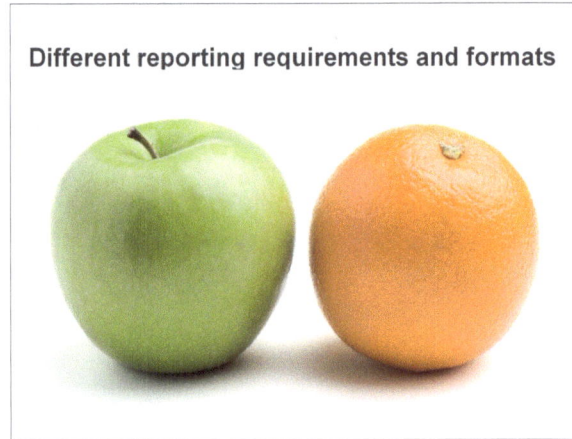

This is the same slide after I learned about slide design. Notice there is now only one idea per slide and the use of 'apples and oranges' as a mental flag.

After learning these new practices, more than one workshop attendee has cursed me for having to stay up late and revise their slides for the following day, like my husband did. But they don't regret the payoff in greater audience engagement.

What About Prezi?

Many workshop participants ask me about Prezi, presentation software that uses motion, zoom, and spatial relationships rather than conventional static slides. When Prezi first launched, many users abandoned it because the zooming feature tended to move in and out too quickly and make viewers motion sick. Being web-based, it can also run slowly if you have a lot of images in your presentation (and you should). However, there is a role for Prezi in innovative reporting particularly when it comes to describing complex systems. The ability of Prezi to zoom in and out to reveal the larger system surrounding a program can be useful for helping stakeholders understand the boundaries included in a system evaluation. Prezi is also good when you want to visually demonstrate taking a deep dive in and out of a topic. But use it wisely.

BLAST OFF
to STELLAR SLIDES

10 strategies to help you DESIGN + DELIVER effective presentations

Learn more about how to create astronomically awesome presentations at stellarslides.com

---

1 NO MORE DEFAULT TEMPLATES!

JUST START WITH WHITE OR GRAY BACKGROUNDS

---

2 Add material ONLY if it has meaning and is conveying super important info.

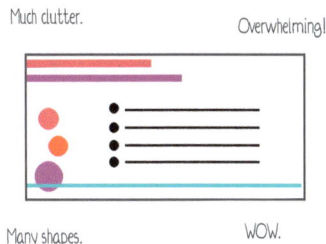

Much clutter. | Overwhelming! | Many shapes. | WOW.

STICK TO GOOD VISUALS, KEY WORDS + DATA

---

3 But don't add SO MUCH TEXT that you don't even need to be there.

LEAVE ONLY A COUPLE KEY WORDS PER SLIDE

---

4 Use information design tricks to make learning EASY for your audience

THESE TRICKS MAKE YOU EASIER TO UNDERSTAND

---

5 For the love of coffee, you don't need BULLET POINTS.

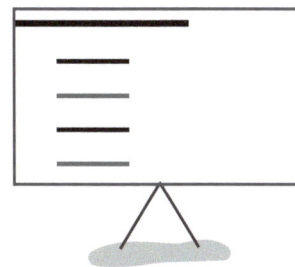

CONTRAST, HIERARCHY + SPACING TO THE RESCUE!

---

6 Good visuals are basically MAGIC!

good visuals | bad visuals
High quality (non lame) stock photos | Small, grainy, stretched out, or distorted photos
Drawings | Random shapes & borders
Icons that don't look like clipart | Clipart -- old or new
Screenshots | Animations

THEY HELP PEOPLE UNDERSTAND + REMEMBER

---

7 ANIMATIONS are usually just confusing clutter, so limit their use.

"APPEAR" IS YOUR BEST GO-TO ANIMATION

---

8 My #1 Tip: 1 to 3 points PER SLIDE.

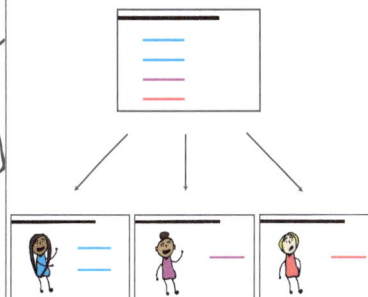

 # OF SLIDES ≠ PRESENTATION LENGTH

---

9 Don't speak AT your audience too long.

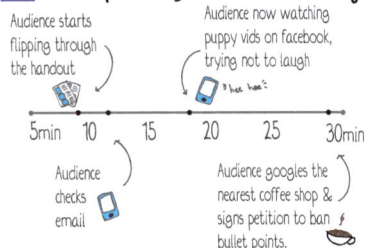

Audience starts flipping through the handout | Audience now watching puppy vids on facebook, trying not to laugh | Audience checks email | Audience googles the nearest coffee shop & signs petition to ban bullet points.

5min 10 15 20 25 30min

BUILD IN BREAKS, QUESTIONS + DISCUSSION

---

10 There is no such thing as PRACTICING too much!

PREPARED PRESENTERS ARE ENGAGING PRESENTERS

"

Best presentation, EVER!

SO engaging!

Way better than coffee!

- your next audience

ECHORIVERA.COM

I love this handy tip sheet from Echo Rivera. You can download it from www.stellarslides.com.[39]

Screencasts

Have you ever experienced this scenario? You've revamped your slides and your presentation down pat. You show up at the assigned time and place, only to find that one or more key managers are unable to attend. I've encountered this situation more times than I care to count and it's so disappointing. It can also be very discouraging from a utilization perspective. Thankfully, you have screencasts as a recourse. A screencast is a digital recording of your slide show with your own audio narration that you record on your computer using regular presentation software. Once you make the recording, it will export as a video file that you can send to stakeholders and display on their computers as a full-screen video.

A screencast is significantly more engaging than a static version of your presentation emailed to absent attendees. Viewers experience all the nuances of your in-person presentation at a time that is convenient to them. Screencasts are also easy to share. Several years ago, I worked with an organization that wanted me to present my evaluation findings to ten different committees. Instead I made one screencast, which they used over and over again as needed.

I usually prepare a script before I get started so my delivery is smoother. Note that 500 words is approximately a three-minute screencast. Ensure you're in as quiet a place as possible to record, and use a headset microphone for better sound quality. If you're practising the technique of layering, you can include a URL on the bottom of the original presentation handout where people can find the screencast later on.

How to Create a Screencast

Power Point 2013 and 2016

1. Select **Slide Show** and **Record Slide Show**.
2. In the **Record Slide Show** box, check **Narrations, Ink, and Laser Pointer**, and click **Start Recording**.
3. To end your recording, right-click the final slide, and click **End Show**.
4. You have two options to save it as a video file:
   a. Save or export your presentation to a video file format such as .mp4 or .wmv.
   b. Save your presentation as a .ppsx file. When someone opens a .ppsx file it appears full-screen in Slide Show on their computer, ready to view immediately.

Keynote for Mac

1. Select **Play**, then **Record Slideshow**.
2. When you are done click **File, Export to**, and then **QuickTime**.

Narrative Summaries

Two-Pagers

One or two-page summaries are one of my favorite reporting methods. Given the choice of writing a fifty-page report or designing a two-page summary, I will always choose the latter. Thankfully, most of my clients prefer reading them too. The examples below show the variety of formats possible in addition to the visual executive summary I shared in Chapter 4. Summaries usually contain a mix of quantitative and qualitative data presented via text, data visualization, and images.

To develop my summaries, I use design software that comes standard on most computers, e.g., Pages for Mac or Microsoft Publisher. But you can put together acceptable summaries with Word too. Over the years I've developed several time-saving templates that I'm able to modify and re-use for new projects. The primary benefit of a short summary is it displays information in smaller, more digestible chunks. Break up the text by using engaging headings (such as your evaluation questions) and plenty of white space. Bold and colored fonts and call-outs will also draw attention to key points.

This one pager from the Idaho Legislature Office of Performance Evaluations communicates the key findings quickly and efficiently.[40]

This one pager from Imagine Canada is not particularly slick, but it's a great substitute (or supplement) to a long report.[41]

I designed this basic two-pager for Whiz Kids International in one day using Pages for Mac and a previous report template.[42]

I gave this two pager to a client along with a ten-minute screencast. It's not super fancy, but it does the job.[43]

When designing a short summary, don't forget to avoid using the standard journal article format, i.e., Introduction, Methods, Results, etc. Think of your summary as an engaging newsletter instead. Which paragraphs will most grab the reader's attention? How can you incorporate the principles of SUCCESs to make it stickier? Try using the condensing technique described on page 30 to determine the flow and content of each paragraph or section.

I'm not a Communications Professional
(But I Play One on TV)

I've struggled with writing succinctly ever since I started replacing my final reports with two-page summaries. I think I can be forgiven for this because as a science major and consultant, I cut my teeth writing long documents like my undergraduate thesis, journal articles, and reports for clients. Sometimes I have Dr. McCoy moments where it feels like I'm pretending to be a communications professional. Just like the old television commercial for Vicks Formula 44 cough syrup where the announcer says, "I'm not a doctor, but I play one on TV."

Let's face it, few evaluators have taken courses in communications or persuasive writing. Since the body of knowledge on effective writing is massive, I've summarized a few quick tips on writing for clarity and simplicity courtesy of The Women's and Children's Health Policy Center.[44]

- Don't use a big word when a smaller one will do.
- Don't use a phrase when a word will do.
- Delete extraneous words or phrases from a sentence whenever possible.
- Use the active voice as much as possible, e.g., "Gill conducted the evaluation," versus "The evaluation was conducted by Gill."
- If you can't quickly identify the subject and verb in a sentence, it is probably too long.

Slidedocs

Slidedocs are a hybrid between a slide presentation and a report popularized by presentation guru, Nancy Duarte.[45] Slidedocs are created using regular slide design programs such as Power Point or Keynote, but they have more detail so users can read them independently as a report. Slidedocs combine blocks of text with images to make them more visually appealing. One advantage of slidedocs over presentations is you can distribute them before a meeting as pre-reading then use the meeting time more effectively to discuss the implications.

Policy Briefs

A policy brief is a persuasive document specifically designed to translate your evaluation evidence into policy and practice. It's an ideal form of report when your intended user is a busy decision maker. A policy brief succinctly describes a problem, its context, and recommendations for action. Most policy briefs are two to four pages long and written using language appropriate for the target audience.

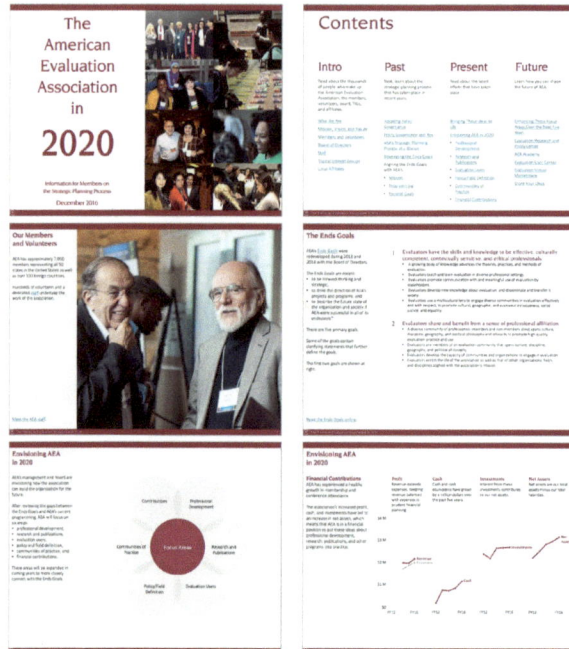

Evaluator Ann Emery created this slidedoc for the American Evaluation Association.[46]

The Women's and Children's Health Policy Center has the following tips on how to write an engaging policy brief.[47]

- Understand your audience before you write.
  - How much exposure do they have to the topic?
  - What is their current technical knowledge of the area?
  - What political or organizational constraints do they face?
  - How open are they to change?
  - What message will most resonate and move them to action?
- Craft a title that is engaging, informative, and answers the question, "Why should I read this?"
- Determine the primary aim of the brief, then write with this in mind. A good policy brief conveys this primary aim in the first minute of reading. (Note that policy briefs are a good place to employ Principal #4 - Reorder Your Key Messages, by summarizing your conclusions and recommendations upfront.)
- State the problem in terms of why it is important to the

audience. Include just enough background information to inform, but not overwhelm, the reader.

- Describe recommended courses of action that are backed by evidence and flow logically from your argument. Specific, concrete recommendations are more effective than abstract ones which can sometimes be open to alternative interpretation.

- Remember that some people will only read the recommendations.

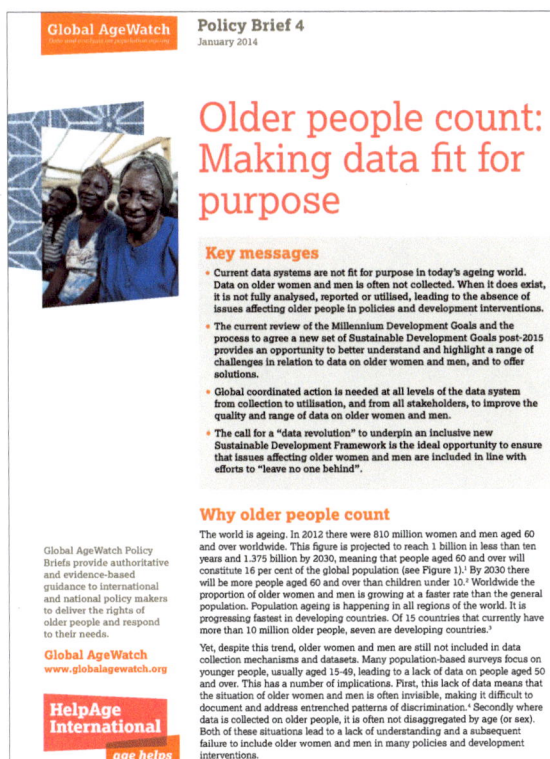

I like the way this policy brief puts the key messages up front.[48]

Newsletters

An effective way to disseminate your findings to the broader public is to write a short article for an organization's own newsletter like the example on the following page. Or if the evaluation is a large one, you can design a newsletter entirely devoted to the evaluation. Recall from Chapter 2 how the survey of evaluators found that the practice of communicating findings to stakeholders as an evaluation progresses strongly influences use. Unlike a policy brief that would be published only after the evaluation is complete, newsletter articles can be published multiple times during the evaluation cycle to keep stakeholders apprised of the evaluation's progress.

This newsletter contains just one paragraph about the evaluation.[49]

This newsletter is entirely devoted to communicating the progress of an evaluation.[50]

Readability

If you've followed Effective Reporting Principle #1—Target Your Audience, and have prepared different types of reports for each stakeholder group, you'll likely want to check the readability of each. Readability is a grade-level indication of the relative complexity of text. You can easily assess readability in Microsoft Word documents by following the steps below.

Windows

1. Click the **File** tab, and then click **Options**.

2. Click **Proofing**.

3. Under **When correcting spelling and grammar in Word**, make sure the **Check grammar with spelling** check box is selected.

4. Select **Show readability statistics**.

Mac

1. On the Word menu, click **Preferences.**

2. Click **Spelling** and **Grammar**.

3. Under **Grammar**, select the **Check grammar with spelling** and **Show readability statistics** check boxes.

4. On the **Tools** menu, click **Spelling and Grammar**. Once Word has finished spell checking the document, it will display the reading level.

Microsoft Word uses the Flesch-Kincaid readability test to indicate reading ease and estimated grade level of the content. You can also find other readability tests online.

Conference Posters

Poster sessions are usually viewed as something just for conference delegates, but why have we limited this form of dissemination only to conferences? Posters can be for offices too. Many of your intended users won't bother to read a final report, but they may glance at an attractively designed poster. Imagine the stickiness of a visually appealing poster hung in an organization's lunch room. If the evaluation results are public, it could even hang in the reception area for greater exposure.

If you've ever attended a conference poster session, you'll know there are a lot of poorly designed posters out there. Below are some tips for developing an engaging poster.[51, 52, 53]

Design

1. Organize your content into sections with clear headings that help orient the reader quickly. Consider using your evaluation questions as headers instead of the traditional Introduction, Methods, Results, etc.

2. Viewers tend to read from top to bottom, so use a column format to vertically structure the flow of your sections. After the title (top and centered), the viewer's attention is most drawn to the top left corner.

3. Keep your poster design neat and clutter free. Avoid lengthy text paragraphs. Aim for 40% white space. Avoid placing borders around text boxes and images, which can interrupt the flow.

4. Opt for dark colored letters on a neutral or light background for better readability. Avoid bright colored backgrounds.

5. Limit your use of colors to two or three. If possible, choose colors that are related to your subject area.

6. Use a font size that is large enough to read from 5-6 feet away. Use a sans serif font for headings and a serif font for body text.

7. Capitalize Each Word of Your Title instead of ALL CAPS for better readability.

8. Do a mock up by printing out each section separately, then lay them out on the floor or large table. Move the segments around to play with different formats and achieve the best flow.

Images

9. Use charts, illustrations, and images to break up large sections of text.

10. Pick relevant and meaningful images that will help to quickly communicate your subject matter. Your own photos are preferable to stock photos, provided they have a high enough resolution (300 dpi).

11. Crop images to include only the most important content.

12. Choose simple and bold illustrations rather than finely detailed ones.

Content

13. Tell a succinct story about your work and why it matters: what you did, what you learned, and what you recommend going forward. The poster should be self-explanatory to someone reading it on their own.

14. Use the sticky note exercise to condense your findings and emphasize your key messages (see *Condensing Your Report* on page 30).

15. State both the question you addressed and your conclusions clearly.

16. Avoid excessive details on the methods you used, unless that is the focus of your topic.

17. Prepare a more detailed one or two-page summary handout as a take-away. Include your contact information.

To the right is an instructional example of an engaging poster.

Tips for Designing Effective Presentations

A poster with the main title in 1½" sans serif

Developed by D. Stong, C. Dwyer, W. Kelty, B. Immel, and K. Winck
with materials donated by Penn State's Education Technology Services

...et the audience's attention ...nd communicate your mes-...age quickly and succinctly.

...tion your images clearly. This is a photo of the design team organizing content: deciding ...t to eliminate, what to keep, and how to arrange it.

...successful poster presents you and ...work clearly and professionally; it ...rages the audience to stop to dis-...the work with you. This text is ¼ ...26 point Times.

...nning

...Keep it simple
...Develop an information hierarchy
...Think visually

Developing a Layout

- The most important things go first.
- Use a grid to keep items aligned and straight.
- Use a text hierarchy.
- Use a column format.
- Try to keep 40% of the poster area empty of text and images.
- Limit your use of boxes and lines.
- If items go together, put them close to each other.

If you look at the image you can find quite a few colors that could be used to create a color scheme for a poster. It's much easier to coordinate a limited number of colors.

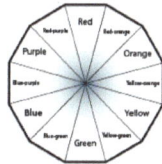

Colors that are near each other on a color wheel go well together.

Selecting Fonts and Using Text

- Use common serif fonts for body text.
- Use sans serif fonts for titles.
- Try to use no more than three fonts.
- Combine both uppercase and lowercase letters.
- Use large fonts that can be easily read from 5 feet away.
- Black text on white has high impact and excellent readability.

Choosing and Using Color

- Maintain a color scheme.
- Keep backgrounds subtle; grays and muted colors help foreground information stand out.
- Use bright, saturated colors sparingly.
- Large amounts of red, yellow or orange can overpower your message.

Serif in Times
AaBbCcDd
AaBbCcDd
Sans Serif in Helvetica

"Serifs" are the little cut-off strokes on letters. "Sans" means "without", so sans serif means without little cut-off strokes.

Be careful that you don't lead the viewer away from your poster. Place the images so that they guide the viewer's eyes to the next bit of information.

Judges Checklist

The following should be clearly presented and readable from a distance of 4 to 6 feet:

1. Title of the exhibit
2. Student's name
3. Collaborators, advisor, and department
4. Funding sources
5. Regulatory committee approval (if the project involves human or animal subjects or biohazardous materials)
6. Objectives
7. Significance to the field
8. Significance to society in general
9. Methods
10. Results
11. Interpretation of results and conclusions
12. Directions for future research

Using Images

- Use meaningful, high-quality images.
- Adjust color and contrast in images.
- Crop or edit images so the important information is obvious.
- Give photos short titles or captions.
- Label directly on maps, charts, and graphs.
- Simplify charts and graphs.
- Use bold lines in graphs so the data can be seen and understood from 5 feet away.
- Place images so that they're balanced visually in the poster and they help to lead the viewer's eye through the material.

Viewers reading this line demonstrate the poster's success!

...ster not only models an engaging poster, but includes lots of valuable tips for designing one too.[54]

Building a Culture of Evaluation
30 Ideas to Apply to Your Organization

INVOLVE STAFF TO INCREASE ENGAGEMENT AND OWNERSHIP

Look for small successes.
Start with simple, informal evaluations to demonstrate benefits and worth

POSITION EVALUATION AS A WAY OF **GIVING STAFF A VOICE**

POSITION EVALUATION AS A WAY OF SHOWING THAT **MANAGEMENT IS LISTENING**

→ Emphasize evaluation is something *they* can direct

→ Evaluate the important outcomes only

→ Emphasize intrinsic motivations, like validation of their effort and transferable skills

Be clear about who the evaluation is for, i.e. YOU and not just the funder

RESOURCE IT APPROPRIATELY

GET COMMUNICATIONS STAFF ON-SIDE
It provides them with positive material to promote the organization

Offer evaluation training to build capacity

Engage expertise in the area of organizational culture change

Identify and recruit evaluation "champions" at the senior levels

Orient new partners to your new focus on evaluation

SCHEDULE TIME UP FRONT
IN THE PROGRAM PLANNING PHASE TO DISCUSS EVALUATION

Inject the term **LEARNING ORGANIZATION** into your persuasion efforts

Decrease the use of jargon
talk about "evaluation questions we want to answer" vs. "outcomes we have to measure"

Demystify "measurement"
Use terms such as "tracking" or "following"

Focus more on **QUALITATIVE DATA,** to acknowledge staff's fears that not everything can be reduced to quantitative

CONSCIOUSLY RECRUIT AND HIRE "EVALUATIVE MINDS"

BRING IN A HIGH PROFILE EVALUATION "EXPERT" TO WORK WITH YOUR ORGANIZATION

Incorporate evaluation into **NEW STAFF ORIENTATIONS**

Acknowledge the **INFORMAL EVALUATION** that staff already does

EMPHASIZE THE BOARD'S ROLE TO REQUEST/DIRECT MORE EVALUATION

Appeal to management's notions of accountability and informed decision-making

Invite senior executives to early evaluation planning meetings to get their perspectives

Incorporate evaluation into **STAFF PERFORMANCE APPRAISALS AND PERSONAL DEVELOPMENT PLANS**

BE SUBVERSIVE AND INFORMALLY COLLECT DATA OF INTEREST TO DEMONSTRATE AREAS NEEDING IMPROVEMENT

MODEL EVALUATION AT EVERY OPPORTUNITY

© 2011 Community Solutions Planning and Evaluation
(www.communitysolutions.ca)

Although it's not a full-size poster, this tip sheet sat on my computer as a plain Word document for years before I asked a graphic designer to redesign it for me. Nowadays, I find it posted on office bulletin boards or pinned by people's desks all over the place. Talk about sticky! You can download it for free from http://www.communitysolutions.ca.

Press Releases

I'm always surprised by how rarely press releases are used to communicate evaluation findings. Sure, they're officially the domain of media communications, but they can also be a great way to disseminate results to the general public. In my experience, few programs think to share their evaluation results this way. This is a shame because as I've already mentioned, research into program sustainability indicates that evidence of impact and a high organizational profile are both associated with increased program longevity.[55] Evaluation is often a good news story that communications staff are hungry for. If you're drafting a press release yourself and have never done one before, there are numerous templates on the web to help you with your first one.

Visuals

Infographics

Infographics have gained a lot of attention over the past few years as a popular communication method for evaluators. An infographic is a visual representation that combines text, images, and data visualizations to explain and tell a story about data. The storytelling feature is what most distinguishes an infographic from an attractive display of charts. From top to bottom, an infographic should take the reader on a journey that increases their understanding of an issue and the data associated with it. Infographics are also very sticky because of their visual content.

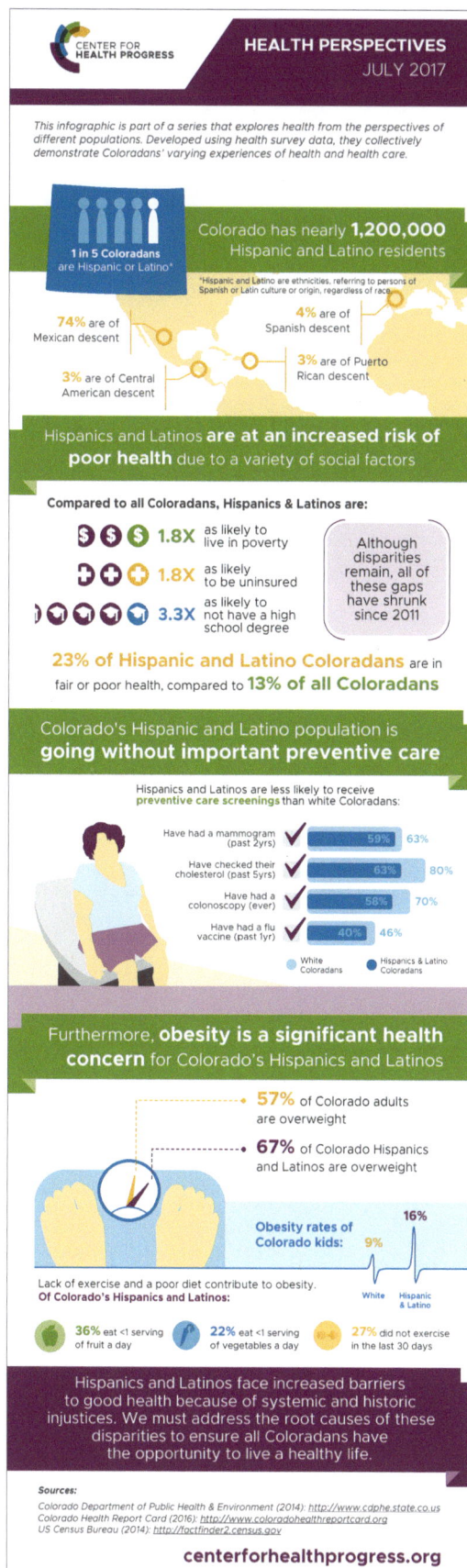

This infographic is attractive and makes its point succinctly.[56]

Be warned, however, that many of the infographics you encounter are created by professional design firms and can be expensive. I've had more than one Dr. McCoy moment reviewing other infographics. Thankfully, several online software programs provide easily customizable templates for producing professional-looking infographics.

Since infographic design is not a standard item in our evaluation toolbox, and one can still make mistakes with templates, evaluator Stephanie Wilkerson has shared her *10 Steps to Creating an Infographic* on the next page.

Some of the more common pitfalls in making infographics are:

- Not having a central purpose or main idea. An infographic is not a data dump.

- Not considering the information needs of your target audience. One infographic might not fit the diverse needs of all your stakeholder groups.

- Not presenting the data accurately. Don't sacrifice rigor for spiffy templates or space restrictions.

- Using a poor color scheme. Stick to three colors. You can find professionally chosen color palettes online on sites such as Adobe Color (https://color.adobe.com/create/color-wheel/).

- Including too much content. Stick to the key messages that illuminate your story.

- Not citing your sources in small print at the bottom. Be sure to include references to increase your infographic's credibility.

This is not your comparison...

Your infographic

All infographics

This is...

Your infographic

Your 250 page report

freshspectrum.com

10 STEPS

Give data a voice by creating infographics with purpose. Follow these steps to communicate a powerful visual story that makes a difference for your audience.

TO CREATING AN INFOGRAPHIC

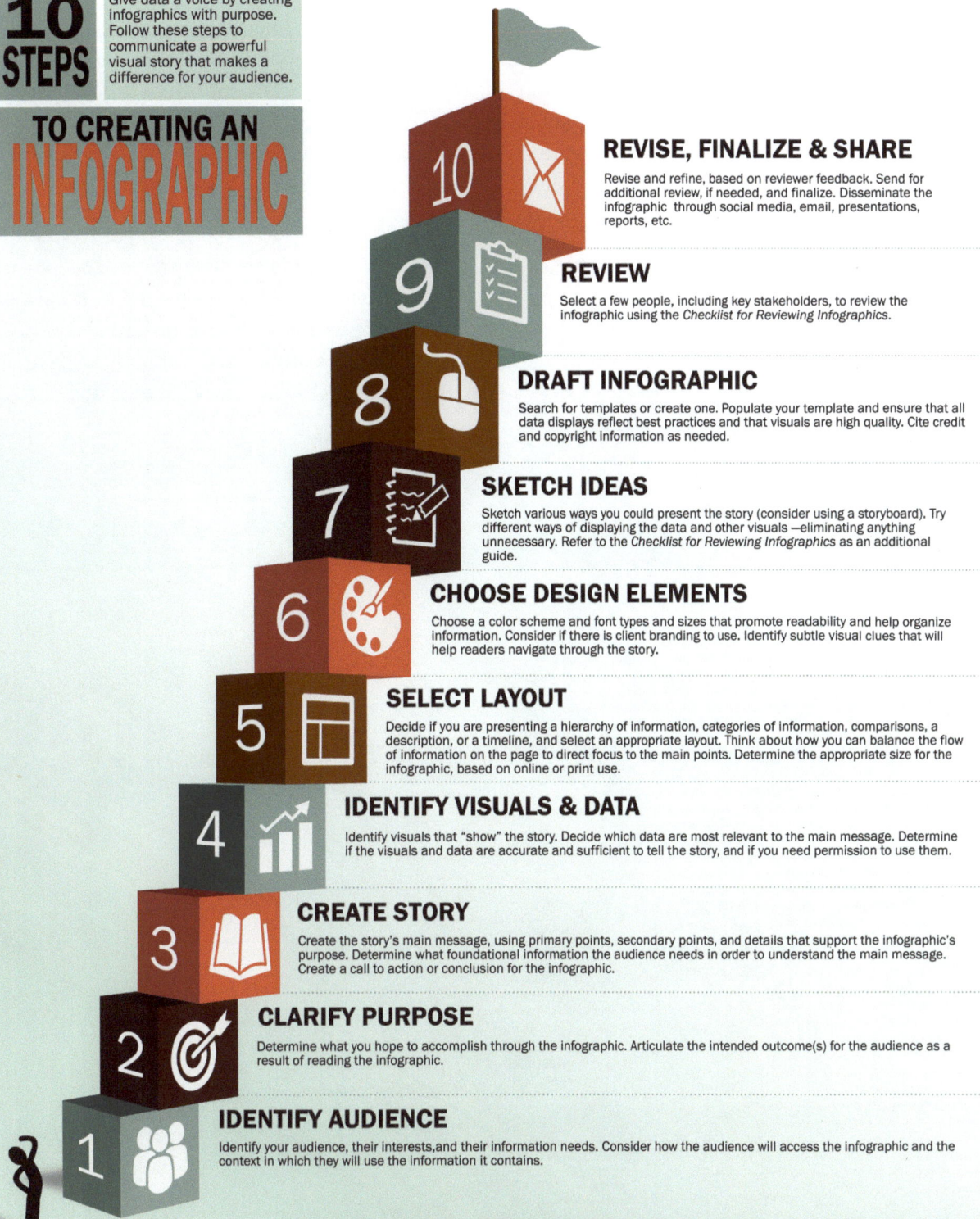

10 REVISE, FINALIZE & SHARE

Revise and refine, based on reviewer feedback. Send for additional review, if needed, and finalize. Disseminate the infographic through social media, email, presentations, reports, etc.

9 REVIEW

Select a few people, including key stakeholders, to review the infographic using the *Checklist for Reviewing Infographics*.

8 DRAFT INFOGRAPHIC

Search for templates or create one. Populate your template and ensure that all data displays reflect best practices and that visuals are high quality. Cite credit and copyright information as needed.

7 SKETCH IDEAS

Sketch various ways you could present the story (consider using a storyboard). Try different ways of displaying the data and other visuals —eliminating anything unnecessary. Refer to the *Checklist for Reviewing Infographics* as an additional guide.

6 CHOOSE DESIGN ELEMENTS

Choose a color scheme and font types and sizes that promote readability and help organize information. Consider if there is client branding to use. Identify subtle visual clues that will help readers navigate through the story.

5 SELECT LAYOUT

Decide if you are presenting a hierarchy of information, categories of information, comparisons, a description, or a timeline, and select an appropriate layout. Think about how you can balance the flow of information on the page to direct focus to the main points. Determine the appropriate size for the infographic, based on online or print use.

4 IDENTIFY VISUALS & DATA

Identify visuals that "show" the story. Decide which data are most relevant to the main message. Determine if the visuals and data are accurate and sufficient to tell the story, and if you need permission to use them.

3 CREATE STORY

Create the story's main message, using primary points, secondary points, and details that support the infographic's purpose. Determine what foundational information the audience needs in order to understand the main message. Create a call to action or conclusion for the infographic.

2 CLARIFY PURPOSE

Determine what you hope to accomplish through the infographic. Articulate the intended outcome(s) for the audience as a result of reading the infographic.

1 IDENTIFY AUDIENCE

Identify your audience, their interests, and their information needs. Consider how the audience will access the infographic and the context in which they will use the information it contains.

Don't forget to use our *Checklist for Reviewing Infographics!*

For this and other resources, visit magnoliaconsulting.org/tools#infographics

magnolia consulting

© 2017 Stephanie B. Wilkerson

This infographic was created by evaluator Stephanie Wilkerson for other evaluators. You can download it from https://magnoliaconsulting.org/tools/#infographics.[57]

Data Dashboards

A data dashboard is an information management and data visualization tool that displays the status of key performance indicators on a single screen. When data dashboards first appeared among evaluators, their popularity was extremely high. Demonstrations at evaluation conferences were standing room only, and everyone was eager to learn more about this compelling tool for reporting.

The purpose of a dashboard is to enable ongoing monitoring, communicate progress at a glance, and guide strategic decision-making. They can be static or interactive. Dashboards excel at presenting dense amounts of data in a clear and succinct fashion. They are not just a communications tool; they can also be used to facilitate participatory data analysis through their ability to interactively drill down into the data.

...more data faster is not what evaluators and their clients need; they need the means to filter the signal from the noise.

Veronica Smith

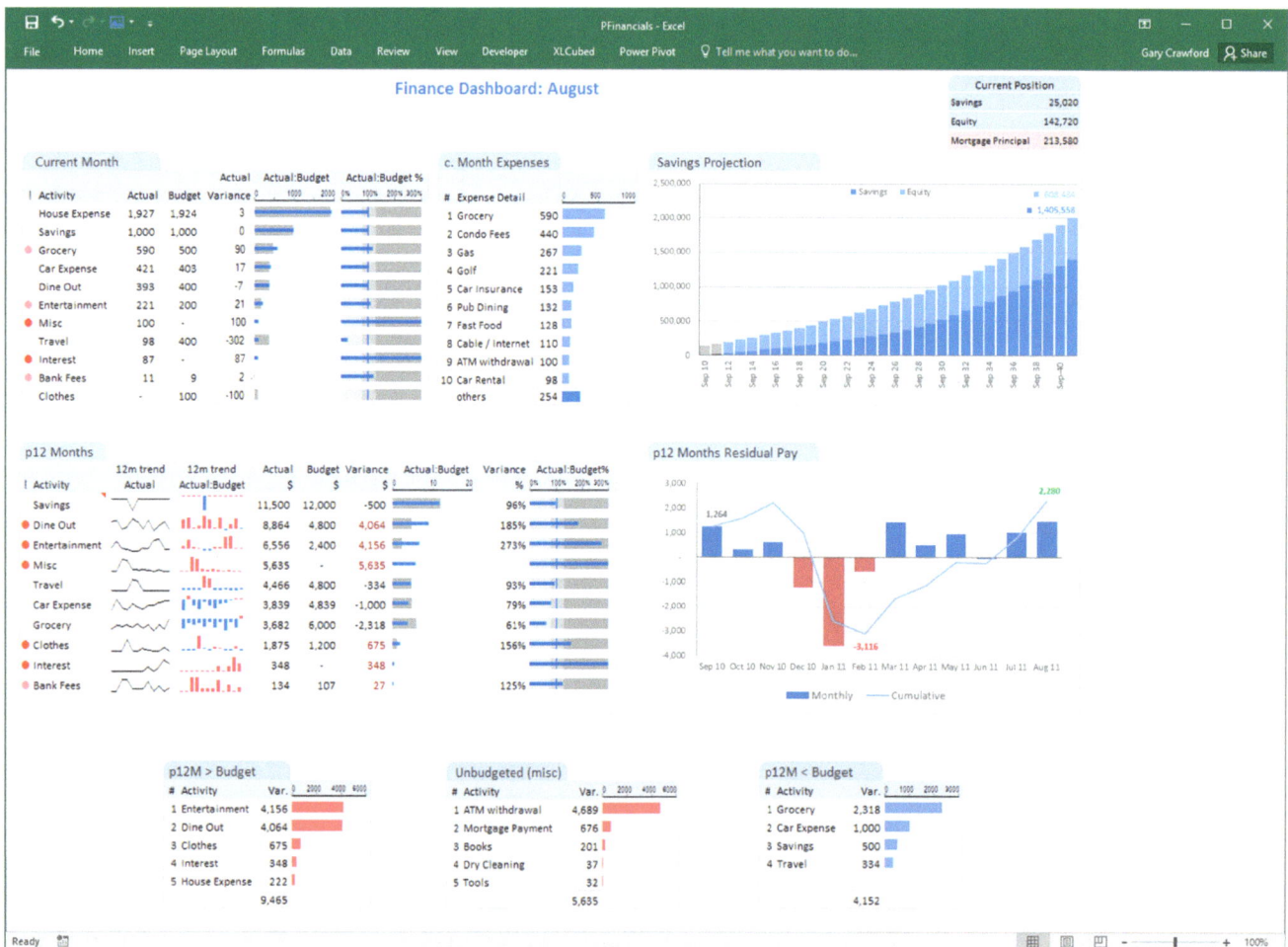

This data dashboard was designed by Gary Crawford using XLCubed.

While there are a number of software programs that allow non-technical users to create a data dashboard, you can also create useful ones in Microsoft Excel. Veronica Smith, who has studied data dashboards for evaluation, has several pieces of advice for designing your dashboard.

1. Be cautious about adding nifty features that detract from the main messages. Software templates aren't necessarily good design choices.

2. Develop and pre-test your dashboard in collaboration with end users for maximum usability and effectiveness.

3. The process of designing a data dashboard involves an investment of time and money, so ensure you budget for both accordingly.[58]

Note that dashboards are primarily quantitative and not very good at communicating things like context or other nuances, which can affect how people interpret the data.[59] Use caution if including long term indicators with high variability over the short-term. Dashboards are also associated with that old cliché, "What gets measured gets done," and can lead stakeholders to ignore emerging outcomes if not careful. Finally, dashboards display metrics that represent strategic priorities, but the assumptions and values used to select these priorities should be transparent and represent the views and needs of all relevant stakeholders.

This dashboard is a solid first step. Can the project team suggest a few tweaks?

No, we could barely afford the initial development.

Flow Charts

Flow charts are frequently used when we're trying to explain a complicated process or theory, but they're more meaningful when stakeholders develop them as a collaborative group.

Sometimes there is nothing quite like a flow chart to help you visually organize your thoughts and ideas. Like logic models. I love logic models. However, I've seen enough flow charts over the years to convince me to avoid using them in my reports. If they become too complex, they can often look like gobbledygook to the unfamiliar reader. In my opinion, a flow chart is only meaningful to the person who developed it. When I come across a flow chart in a report my eyes tend to glaze over and I only glance at it quickly. It may be my particular learning preference, but I would rather learn about a process or theory through its application to a concrete real-life example instead of a visual hodgepodge of shapes and lines.

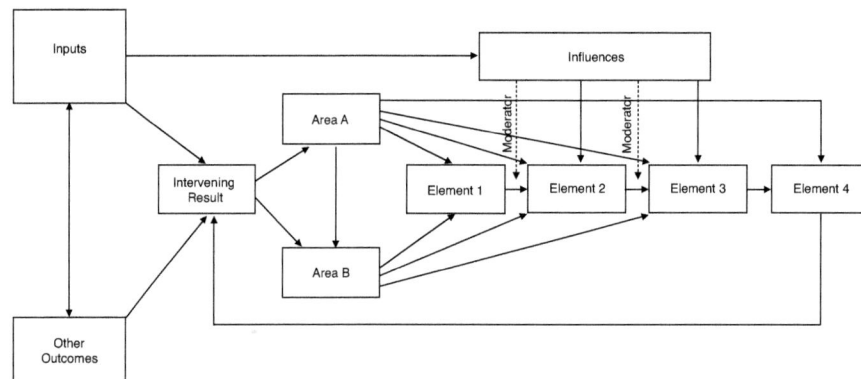

Flow charts are not always meaningful to readers.

However, when everyone plays a part in their development, people understand what each square, circle, and arrow represents. This realization hit me when I once tried to develop a system map for a committee. A system map is a visual tool used to depict complexity. It depicts things like different actors in a system, interrelationships, and feedback loops. I thought my map was amazing and packed full of insights, but when I showed it to the committee nobody understood it. It was some weeks later when I finally grasped that only through drawing the map myself was I able to fully appreciate what it represented. It was the *process* of producing the map that yielded the insights, not simply staring at the *product*.

In my experience, when it comes to diagrams like flow charts and system maps, the process of developing them is more useful than the diagram itself.

Mapping

Nowhere is the axiom, "A picture is worth a thousand words," perhaps more relevant in evaluation than the use of maps in final reports. Notice how the following examples quickly communicate impacts or gaps in service to readers. Customizing a Google Map like the example to the right is relatively easy. If you wish to do something more advanced using GIS (Geographic Information System), you will likely need to contract with someone who has expertise in this area.

A customized Google Map is useful for demonstrating gaps in service in neighborhoods.

Symbols for various early childhood programs quickly highlight which neighborhoods are lacking in services.[60]

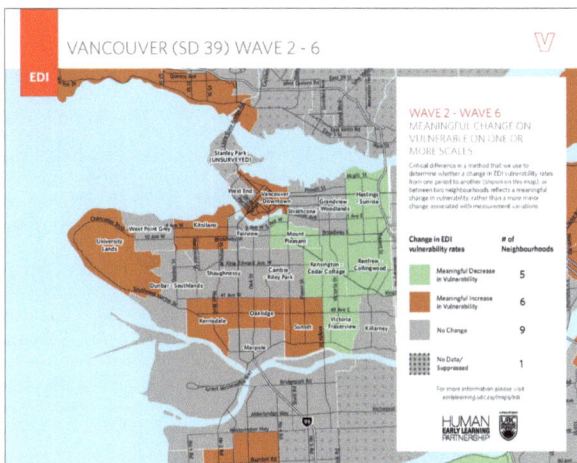

This map uses color to indicate neighborhoods demonstrating a meaningful change over time in early childhood development vulnerability scores.[61]

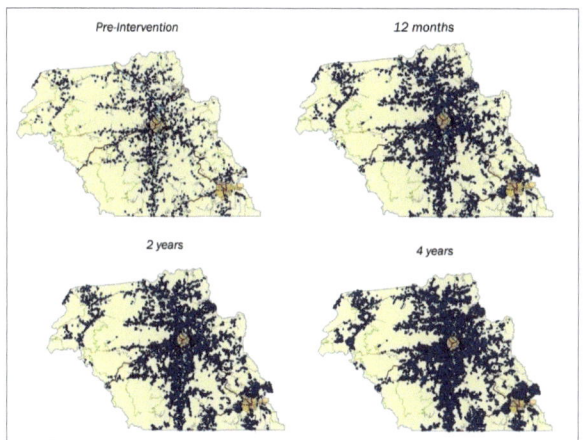

Stephen C. Maack and Arlene Hopkins showed me at an AEA workshop how GIS mapping can be used to quickly communicate changes in outcomes over time. I adapted the labels on this example from Carla Norwood to illustrate how it can be done.[62]

Graphic Recording

Graphic recording is a visual activity that combines words and images to create a conceptual map of a conversation. During a meeting or other event, a trained (and usually silent) graphic facilitator works at the front of the room to draw a large-scale visual record of the discussion in real-time. The resulting mural is a permanent and highly engaging record of the discussion that has taken place.

Graphic facilitation is particularly useful during participatory sessions such as evaluation planning or data parties. What I like most about these murals is they're very sticky. I've seen them displayed in lunchrooms and office hallways weeks after an event, providing a long-term reminder of the key ideas raised.

A graphic recording Kat Haugh created in August 2016 with the USAID LEARN Contract for a group of USAID staff called the "Learning Dojo." [63]

Cartoons and Comics

Cartoons (one panel) and comics (sequential panels) can be a fun and engaging way to effectively make your point with stakeholders. Remember, novelty makes your results stickier in the minds of decision makers. There are numerous sites online that allow you to quickly develop your own. Choose your background, select your characters, think of a funny situation that emphasizes your key message and bingo! You have a cartoon or comic. If you're feeling ambitious, you might consider a longer graphic novel. It's certainly been done at least once for a doctoral dissertation. If you want something more sophisticated, you can find people to design reasonably priced custom cartoons and comics on websites such as Fiverr (http://www.fiverr.com) or Freelancer (http://www.freelancer.com).

I created this comic online in less than an hour.

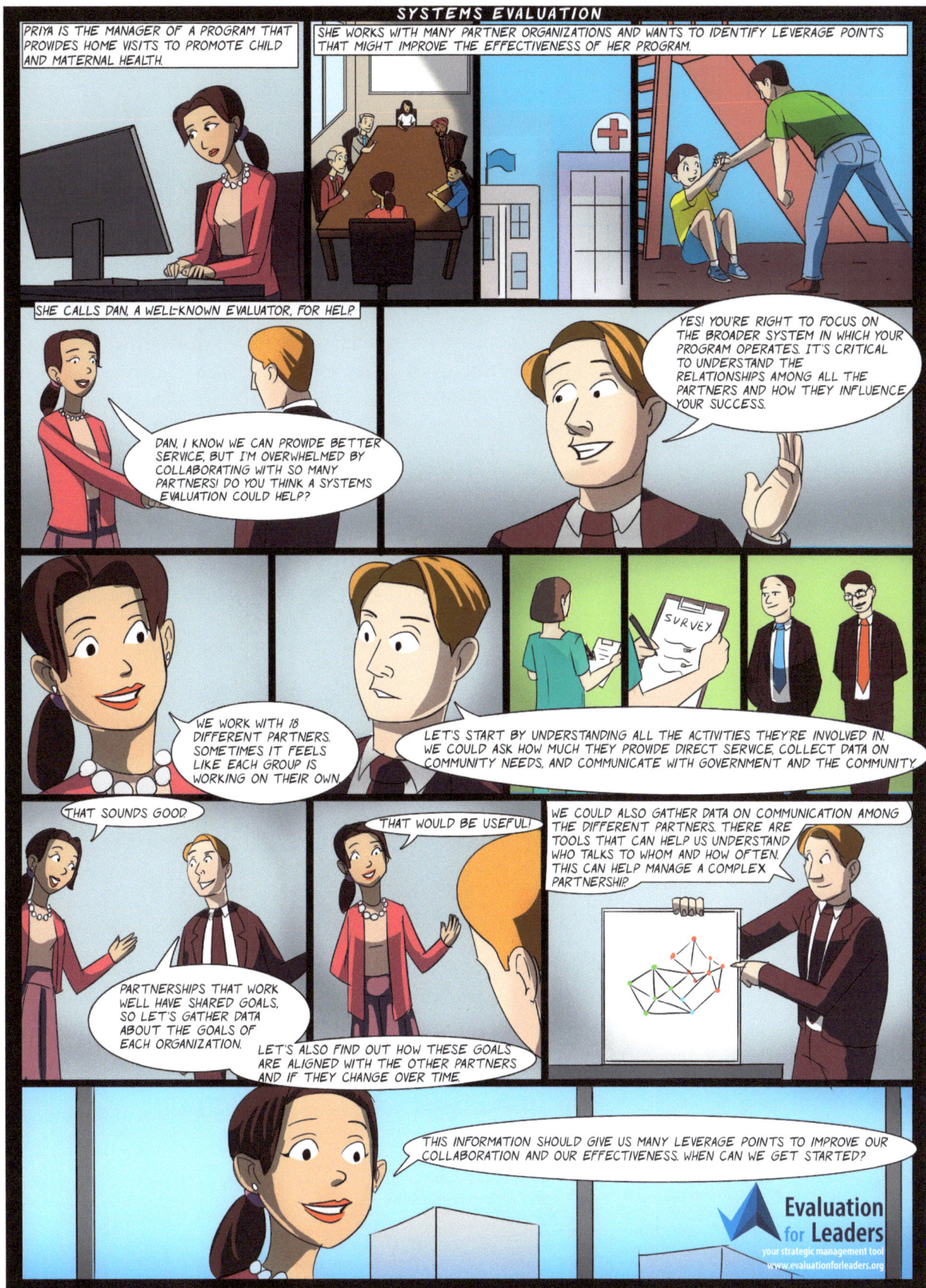

I contracted a graphic artist to develop this custom comic from a script I provided. This was not nearly as expensive as you might think.

Digital

Animated Videos

Many evaluators have used YouTube videos to present their results. Another great option is an Explainer video. Explainer videos, such as the example below, are all the rage these days and for good reason. In under three minutes they have the power to convey complex results and concepts in a way that grabs and keeps stakeholders' attention. You can make your own simple animated videos using free online sites, or contract a design professional. The Curse of Knowledge can make keeping your content to under three minutes a challenge. However, if you use the condensing technique discussed on page 30 you will make a good start.

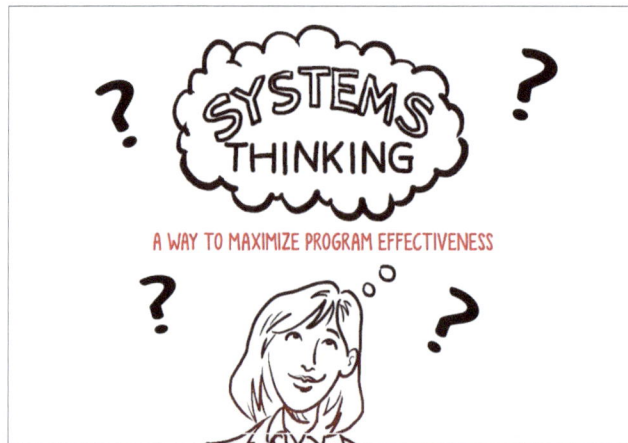

Bev Parsons, Chris Lovato, and I contracted a whiteboard video maker to produce this Explainer video.[64]

Interactive Websites

The best example I know of an interactive website used for evaluation reporting is the Oregon Paint Stewardship Pilot Program evaluation. This website opens with a visual overview of the paint lifecycle. When users click a paint splatter, a new window pops up with tabbed multimedia options for viewing the evaluation questions, data collection methods, and key findings. In my opinion, this website is a great example of an interactive evaluation report, although I recognize the budget to develop it was likely significant.

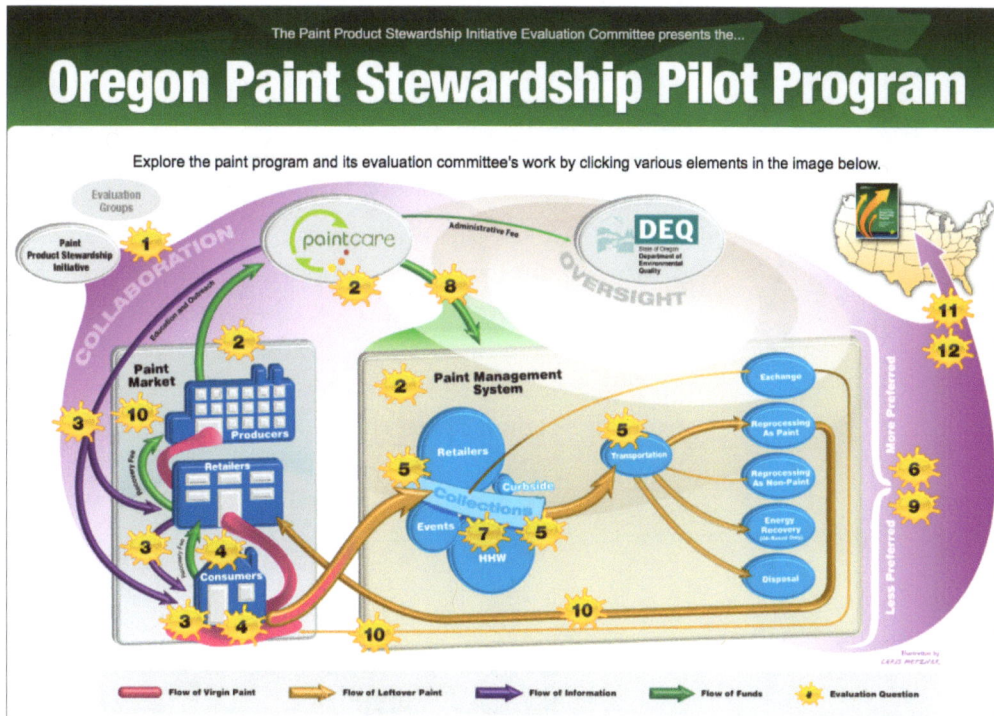

You can explore all the features of this interactive online evaluation report at http://www.paintstewardshipprogram.com.[65]

Email Marketing

Why not use email marketing to communicate your findings? Many of us send our reports to stakeholders as a PDF attachment, but these can languish for weeks or months in people's inboxes. The campaigns created by email marketing websites such as MailChimp, Constant Contact, and AWeber are colorful and engaging. Their standard format (several short paragraphs with links to learn more) are a great opportunity to use the principle of layering. Best of all, email newsletters are easy to produce. Choose one of the templates provided, customize the colors and logo, then add your content, images, and links. Just be sure to select a template that is mobile friendly, as more than half of email opens these days are on a mobile device.[66]

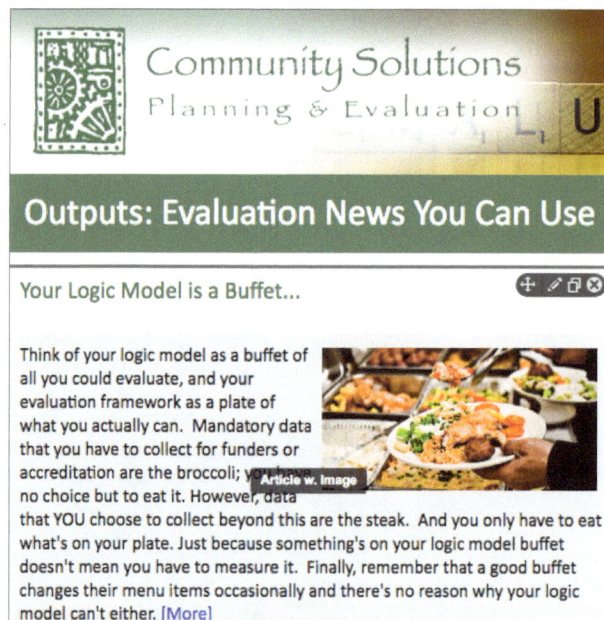

I created this email using a template from Constant Contact. Notice the use of layering with a link to more information.

Podcasts

A podcast is a digital audio file that stakeholders can listen to whenever and wherever they want. There are podcasts on just about any topic. Evaluators are starting to embrace this form of communication as well. MEASURE Evaluation offers several podcasts as does the US Government Accountability Office. What excites me the most about podcasts is their potential to grab the attention of busy managers while they're out for a jog, on a flight, or during their daily commute. For years I wanted to read Peter Senge's *Fifth Discipline*, but at the end of a long day, it never looked very appealing on my bedside table. But when I downloaded it as an audiobook for an evaluation book club, I listened to it in a week just walking to my office.

You can record a podcast with just yourself talking, or set it up as an interview with another colleague or program recipient to make it more engaging. There are free audio editing programs online to ensure you create a high-quality recording such as Audacity (http://www.audacity.com), and you can host them via sites such as SoundCloud (http://www.soundcloud.com).*

You might consider some of the next few ideas a little too radical for your taste, but that's okay. Start where you're comfortable, and keep an open mind that some of them are surprisingly effective in certain contexts.

Physical Items

The items in this section range from a data wheel and data cube, to fortune cookies and a cootie catcher. The primary advantage of using physical items such as these is they have the potential to hang around an office on a desk, bulletin board, or even the back of bathroom stalls, hence making them stickier.

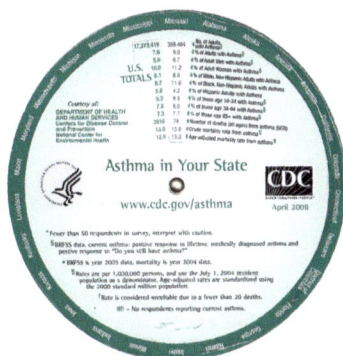

The CDC's National Asthma Control Program used a rotating wheel device to present a substantial amount of data in an engaging way.

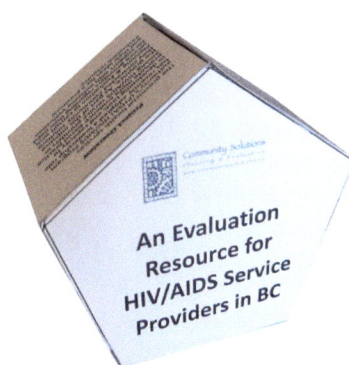

This data cube summarizes key messages and can sit on a policy maker's desk. To make your own data cube, see the template in the Appendix, or download from www.communitysolutions.ca.

---

* Although they're not reports per se, two podcasts by and for evaluators on general evaluation topics are Adventures in Evaluation (https://adventuresinevaluation.podbean.com) and Eval Café (https://evalcafe.wordpress.com).

Stephanie Evergreen suggests engaging stakeholders by baking key findings into fortune cookies.[67]

Stephanie also came up with this innovative idea of a scratch-off graph using clear packing tape and scratch-off paint.[68]

I love this cootie catcher sent to me by past workshop participant, Brandie Ward.

Susan Kistler came up with this idea of adding key messages to a Hershey Kiss.

Evaluation Poetry

We tried to increase school nutrition,
But our goals didn't come to fruition,
Because candy machines,
Are more favoured by teens,
We'll address this the next edition.

Poetry, Drama, and Dance

At the 2004 American Evaluation Association conference in Atlanta, I almost fell off my chair when respected evaluators Hallie Preskill and Rosalie Torres presented a session on using poetry, drama, and other creative pursuits for reporting. *Well, well,* I thought, *the sky is really the limit here.* While these artistic methods won't suit all types of evaluation, you might have an opportunity to incorporate this level of creativity into your reports, depending on your context. Take a look at the following examples.

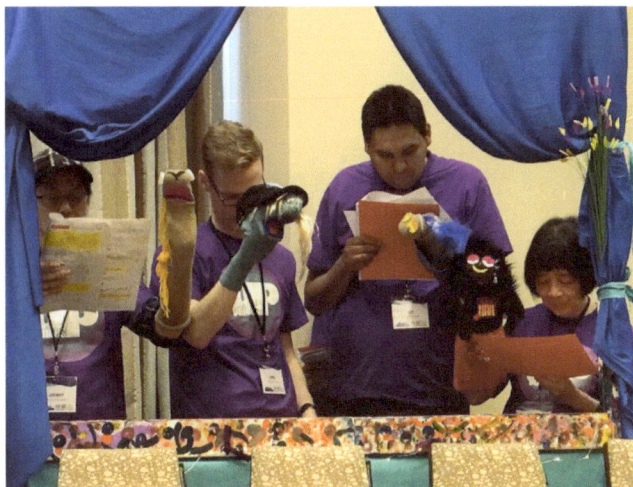

A scene from Voices UP!, a play collectively created at the UBC Learning Exchange that used puppets as a tool for evaluation and results sharing.[69]

For years I used to joke in my workshops about using interpretive dance as a final report, until Charné Furcron showed me how it's actually done! You can view it at http://bit. do/ADTAdancereport.[70]

If you're concerned about evaluation utilization, I've just given you more than twenty alternatives for innovative reports that you can use instead of, or in addition to, the traditional final report. These ideas are just a sample of the ever-expanding range of possibilities coming to the fore as evaluators young and old continue to push the envelope. The sky is truly the limit, but remember not to sacrifice accuracy for novelty. We are still evaluators after all.

Hopefully you're feeling super inspired right now. But if you still feel intimidated, or are having a Dr. McCoy moment, don't worry because I have some tips for you in the next chapter.

Chapter Summary

- There are numerous innovations that can be used in place of, or in addition to, the traditional long report.

- Simple public speaking tips can dramatically improve the effectiveness of oral presentations.

- Engaging slides are characterized by six or fewer words, no bullets, clutter free and light-colored backgrounds, full-bleed high-quality images, and one idea per slide.

- Examples of narrative summaries are two pagers, slidedocs, policy briefs, newsletters, posters, and press releases.

- Visual alternatives include infographics, data dashboards, maps, graphic recording, cartoons, and comics.

- Examples of digital options are animated videos, interactive videos, email marketing, and podcasts.

- Other possibilities for certain audiences are poetry, drama and dance.

Chapter 6 - Moving Forward

Despite the current popularity for innovative reporting, evaluators often tell me the pace of change is glacial in some organizations, both large and small. I regularly hear people bemoan the institutional restraints placed on their reporting. Things like mandatory slide templates and lengthy report policies can prevent evaluators from focusing on what really matters, which is the dissemination and use of the findings.

Everett Rogers' *Diffusion of Innovation Theory,*[71] is often used to examine the spread and adoption of new ideas. If we consider how practices in evaluation reporting are changing, many evaluators and the organizations they work with have moved beyond "The Big Scary Chasm in Question" in the figure below. Where are you? And where are some of the organizations you work with? If you're not where you want to be, here are some ideas to facilitate the adoption of more innovative alternatives under challenging circumstances.

LEARNING OBJECTIVE

After reading this chapter, you will be able to:

• Explain ways to facilitate the adoption of innovative reporting in non-receptive environments.

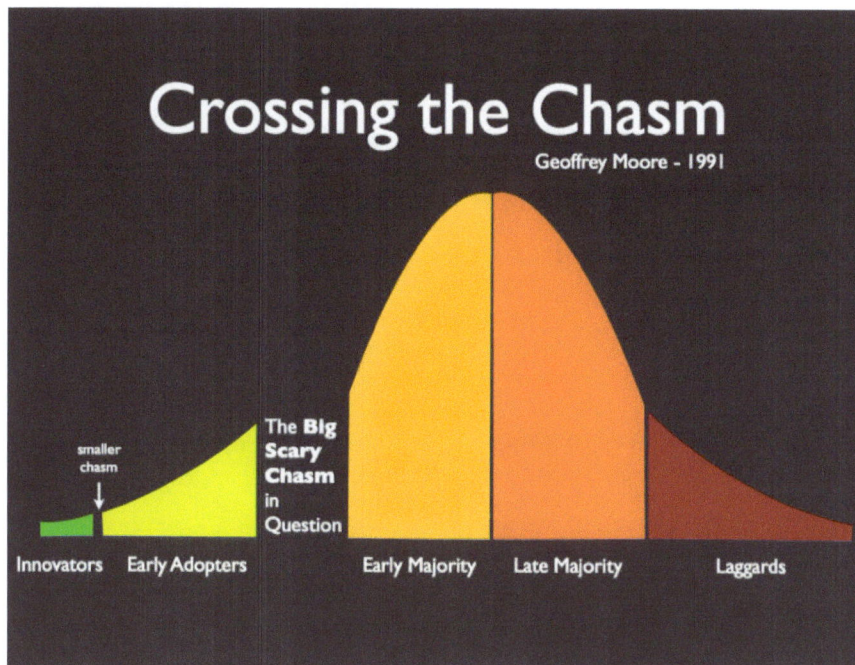

Where are you and the organizations you work with located on this chart?[72]

Be Subversive

Don your camouflage fatigues folks, because I'm about to give you instructions on how to be subversive with your evaluation reporting.

- **Don't ask for permission, ask for forgiveness.** When it comes to innovative alternatives, many managers don't know what they don't know. Instead of asking for permission to try something new, produce it first and then show it to your manager. An actual product or prototype will be more likely to convince them than a verbal description.

- **Use peer pressure.** Consider mentioning formal initiatives that are actively trying to change evaluators' thinking in this area such as the American Evaluation Association's Potent Presentations Initiative, eStudies and webinars, or the Data Visualization Topical Interest Group's conference slide clinics. You can even show them this book.

Instead of asking for permission to try something new, produce it first and then show it to your manager.

Baby Steps

Remember that your efforts don't have to be super slick. I recommend taking baby steps and starting with something small to increase your confidence (and perhaps that of your manager's). Start with a one page fact sheet rather than an expensive and complicated interactive dashboard. If you're still feeling uncertain, focus on the fifty-page document that your stakeholders will *not* receive and pat yourself on the back for putting stakeholder engagement and utilization ahead of an outdated practice.

Kylie Hutchinson @EvaluationMaven · Feb 3

Bringing a new funder up-to-speed on an #eval. Told her the previous reports are only 3 pages long. The relief in her voice was palpable.

♡ ⟲ ♡ 9 ✉

Outsource Assistance

If, along the way, you find yourself having several Dr. McCoy moments, remember you don't have to do it all. You don't have to become an expert in graphic design overnight. In fact, you don't have to become an expert at all. Determine where your strengths lie and consider outsourcing to a sub-contractor when you need help. Although I've been exploring innovative reporting for almost ten years, I've never had the time to develop a data dashboard myself. If the opportunity does arise, I'll likely have to hire someone to help me. You might be fortunate to work in a location where communication and other expertise is already available to you in-house. If not, select one or two new skills that you want to improve and slowly pick away at these.

The Ever-Expanding Evaluation Toolbox

When I did my first evaluation in 1988, my primary focus was on my statistical skills and using rigorous methods. When I became an independent consultant in 1997 and started working with nonprofits, I learned the importance of being a good program planner. Adopting a participatory evaluation approach had me taking courses in group facilitation and consensus-building. When I became interested in evaluation capacity-building, I got a certificate in adult education and instructional design. Learning about evaluation reporting and utilization had me researching communication techniques, and the advent of data visualization forced me to spend time reading about graphic design. When I practiced monitoring and evaluation in Africa, new developments in mobile data collection required me to improve my technical skills. The growing field of systems evaluation now has me sharpening my system thinking skills. These days, I also spend a lot of time pondering the role of the evaluator in organizational development and change management.

Whoa.

Although I love all these innovations, my evaluator's toolbox is starting to get full. As our field becomes more and more specialized, it gets harder to be a jack-of-all-trades. The solution for many of us is to get help. Determine your strengths and outsource your weaknesses. Pick several areas you want to learn more about and ask for assistance with the others.

Evaluation reporting is growing at a rapid pace, but not every evaluator is able to implement these new ideas in their workplace. By being slightly subversive, taking baby steps, and outsourcing as necessary, you and the organizations you work with can begin to experiment with more innovative reporting and drive greater utilization.

Chapter Summary

- The field of evaluation has started to embrace innovative reporting in a significant way.

- Although some evaluators face organizational restrictions on their reporting practices, several techniques can help encourage the adoption of alternatives under challenging circumstances.

- Instead of asking for permission to try something new, produce an actual prototype first to better convince a manager.

- Take baby steps and start with something small to increase your confidence. Remember your efforts don't have to be slick.

- If something feels beyond your current skill set, consider outsourcing to a professional.

Conclusion

When I gave my first workshop on evaluation reporting back in 2008, little did I realize I was on the cusp of a revolution in how evaluators disseminate their findings. Back then, some of the ideas in Chapter 5 were considered unconventional and downright radical. Nowadays, people have changed their opinions drastically. From infographics to podcasts, and newsletters to cartoons, evaluators everywhere are challenging the status quo of the final report.

In this short primer, I've highlighted the need for greater innovation in evaluation reporting, introduced you to four principles to guide better reporting, showed you how to make your key messages stickier, listed simple ways to improve upon the traditional final report, and described more innovative alternatives. This book is simply the tip of the iceberg, but I hope it has left you feeling inspired.

If we practice more effective reporting, we will better engage our stakeholders. If we can better engage our stakeholders, we'll see greater use of our findings. If there is greater use of our findings, just imagine the change we can spark.

But don't take my word for it, try it yourself on your next evaluation.

For additional tips, ideas, and techniques, visit the Evaluation Reporting Pinterest page at https://www.pinterest.com/evaluationmaven/evaluation-reporting/.

REFLECT

Take a moment to think about everything we've discussed in this primer. What new techniques or formats are you going to try?

If we practice more effective reporting, we will better engage our stakeholders.

If we can better engage our stakeholders, we'll see greater use of our findings.

If there is greater use of our findings, just imagine the change we can spark.

Appendix A - Data Parties

You're invited to a
DATA PARTY!

Who? → YOU AND YOUR KEY STAKEHOLDERS

What? → A GATHERING THAT ALLOWS PEOPLE TO INTERACT WITH AND INCREASE THEIR UNDERSTANDING OF YOUR DRAFT FINDINGS, AND PROVIDE INPUT INTO FINAL CONCLUSIONS AND RECOMMENDATIONS. ALSO KNOWN AS PARTICIPATORY SENSE-MAKING, RESULTS-BRIEFINGS, AND PARTICIPATORY DATA ANALYSIS.

When? → BEFORE YOU DRAFT THE FINAL REPORT.
ALLOW FOR TWO HOURS MINIMUM.

Why? → PEOPLE SUPPORT WHAT THEY HELPED TO CREATE!

Where? → IN A SMALL GROUP, LARGE FORUM, OR ONLINE MEETING. IT'S UP TO YOU!

How? → POSE REFLECTIVE QUESTIONS ABOUT THE FINDINGS TO THE GROUP SUCH AS:
WHAT IS THIS DATA TELLING YOU?
WHAT DO YOU THINK IS OCCURRING HERE, AND WHY?
HOW DOES IT ALIGN WITH YOUR EXPECTATIONS?
IS THIS BETTER OR WORSE THAN YOU EXPECTED?
WHAT REALLY STANDS OUT FOR YOU?
ARE THERE ANY SURPRISES HERE?
WHAT RESPONSE DO YOU THINK IS REQUIRED HERE?
HOW VIABLE ARE THESE RECOMMENDATIONS?
WHICH FEEL MOST DOABLE?
HOW MIGHT WE BEST COMMUNICATE THESE FINDINGS TO DECISION-MAKERS?

Community Solutions
Planning & Evaluation
www.communitysolutions.ca
©2016

Appendix B - Recommendations
That Rock

RECOMMENDATIONS THAT ROCK!

TRANSLATE YOUR EVALUATION FINDINGS INTO **ACTION** BY CRAFTING RECOMMENDATIONS THAT REFLECT **SOME OR ALL OF** THE FOLLOWING CHARACTERISTICS:

SPECIFIC
MEASUREABLE
ACHIEVABLE
RESULTS-ORIENTED
TIME-BOUND

⇨ DERIVED DIRECTLY FROM EVALUATION FINDINGS

⇨ DIRECTLY LINKED TO THE EVALUATION PURPOSE

⇨ DIRECTLY LINKED TO THE EVALUATION QUESTIONS

⇨ HAVE BEEN VETTED BY STAKEHOLDERS

⇨ WITHIN SCOPE OF CONTROL OF INTENDED USERS

ARE CATEGORIZED MEANINGFULLY

By » PRIORITY » TIMING » EVALUATION QUESTION
» PROGRAM ASPECT » STAKEHOLDER GROUP
» TYPE OF ACTION REQUIRED

★ BEGIN WITH A STRONG ACTION VERB

★ DON'T RESTATE THE CONCLUSIONS

★ BRIEFLY SUMMARIZE THE EVIDENCE

★ INDICATE WHO IS SUPPOSED TO ACT

★ SUGGEST DIFFERENT AVENUES FOR IMPLEMENTATION

★ PROVIDE SUFFICIENT DETAIL FOR FOLLOW—THROUGH

★ ESTIMATE COSTS OF IMPLEMENTATION

★ SPECIFY POTENTIAL BENEFITS

★ TREAT DELICATE ISSUES SENSITIVELY

AND

REALISTIC

UNBIASED

FACT-BASED

With acknowledgment to Lori Wingate, Michael Hendricks, and Meredith Papagiannis.

Community Solutions
Planning & Evaluation
www.communitysolutions.ca
©2015

Appendix C - Checklist for Program Evaluation Report Content

EvaluATE

Checklist for Program Evaluation Report Content
Kelly N. Robertson and Lori A. Wingate | October 2017

This checklist identifies and describes the elements of an evaluation report. It is intended to serve as a flexible guide for determining an evaluation report's content. It should not be treated as a rigid set of requirements. An evaluation client's or sponsor's reporting requirements should take precedence over the checklist's recommendations. Decisions about the order of content and level of detail in a report should be made with consideration of the audience's information needs and priorities.

This checklist is strictly focused on the *content of long-form technical evaluation reports*. Although important, alternative reporting methods (e.g., infographics and slide decks) and visual elements (e.g., document design and data visualization) are outside the scope of this checklist.

This checklist is designed to guide the development of *project* or *program* evaluation reports. For the sake of readability, we use the term *program* to mean either projects or programs. The checklist is not intended to assist in the writing of product, policy, or personnel evaluation reports.

A one-page summary is provided at the end of this checklist.

TITLE PAGE
The title page provides basic information about the report's content.

- ☐ **Title:** Provide a succinct, informative name for the report. Include the word *evaluation;* program name; and report timing, such as annual, midterm, or final report.

- ☐ **Recipient(s):** Identify the name, title, organization, and contact information of the individual(s) to whom the report is being submitted.

- ☐ **Author(s):** Identify the name, title, organization, and contact information of the individual(s) who wrote the report. (If the person submitting the report is different from the author, identify that person separately.)

- ☐ **Date:** Identify the month and year when the report was completed.

- ☐ **Preferred citation:** Provide complete reference information so that others may cite the report. Include the author, year, title, and web address, if available (example on page 5).

ACKNOWLEDGMENTS
The acknowledgements section identifies and thanks individuals who directly or indirectly assisted or facilitated the evaluation process.

- ☐ **Contributors:** Identify each person by name. If desired, identify their specific contributions.

TABLE OF CONTENTS
The table of contents is a list of the report's main components, which helps readers locate specific items of interest.

- ☐ **Headings:** List all first- and second-level headings, including the titles of all documents in the appendices.

- ☐ **Page numbers:** Identify the page numbers on which each of these components begins.

LIST OF TABLES AND FIGURES
Include a list of tables and figures when there are five or more in a report.

- ☐ **Titles:** List the exact titles of all tables and figures.

- ☐ **Page numbers:** Identify the page numbers on which each table and figure begins.

LIST OF ACRONYMS
Include a list of acronyms if five or more appear in the report. This list helps readers locate acronym definitions.

- ☐ **Definitions:** List acronyms alphabetically and identify the terms they represent.

---

www.evalu-ate.org | Western Michigan University

EXECUTIVE SUMMARY

The executive summary is a synopsis of key information from the main report. This section usually includes important findings, conclusions, and recommendations. The executive summary tends to be the most widely read part of a report. Since it may be the only section some individuals read, it should make sense when read apart from the main report.

☐ **Most important content:** Highlight key content from the report, based on the needs of the report's main audiences.

INTRODUCTION

The introduction orients the reader to the type of information included in the report.

☐ **Overview:** Identify the program that was evaluated and what the report is about.

☐ **Structure:** Describe how the report's content is organized.

☐ **Intended audience:** Identify the groups or individuals for whom the report was developed.

☐ **Purpose and intended use:** Briefly note why the evaluation was conducted and how the results are intended to be used.

PROGRAM DESCRIPTION

The program description section includes details about the program that was evaluated to help readers understand the context of the evaluation's implementation and results.

☐ **Goals and/or objectives:** Identify the specific achievements the program is designed to bring about.

☐ **Funder and funding:** Identify the entities that sponsor the program and the total program budget. Note any significant in-kind contributions.

☐ **Organizations involved:** Identify organizations involved in the program and their roles.

☐ **Intended beneficiaries:** Identify the groups or types of individuals the program is designed to serve.

☐ **Program design:** Describe the program's activities and how they are supposed to bring about desired changes. If the program has a logic model or theory of change, include it here. If the program is based on established theories or literature, identify and describe those as well.

☐ **Context:** Describe relevant economic, political, environmental, cultural, social, or other important factors that influence the conditions in which the program operates.

☐ **History:** Identify the program's stage of maturity, such as whether it is a new initiative, has been operating for a long time, or is winding down for closure. Describe how the program has changed over time.

EVALUATION BACKGROUND

The evaluation background section identifies key factors that influenced the evaluation's planning and implementation. This section helps readers understand the general orientation of the evaluation and the opportunities and constraints that affected decisions about the evaluation.

☐ **Purpose and intended use:** Identify why the evaluation was conducted, such as to meet funder requirements. Describe how the results are intended to be used, such as to inform program improvement.

☐ **Scope:** Identify the boundaries of the evaluation in terms of time period, location, and the specific program components that were evaluated.

☐ **Stakeholder engagement:** Describe how stakeholders were involved in and influenced the evaluation's planning and implementation—beyond serving as data sources.

☐ **Responsiveness to culture and context:** Describe the steps taken to ensure the evaluation was culturally responsive and tailored to context.

☐ **Budget:** Identify the total funding for the evaluation and the percentage of the overall program budget it constituted.

☐ **Evaluation team:** Briefly describe the composition of the evaluation team and each member's role. Describe the degree to which the evaluation team was internal and/or external to the program being evaluated. Disclose any real or perceived conflicts of interest—relationships or factors that could affect the credibility of the evaluation—and describe how they were managed.

☐ **Prior evaluation:** If the program has been evaluated before, summarize key takeaways and implications for the current evaluation.

EVALUATION METHODS

The evaluation methods section describes how the evaluation was implemented and how the evaluation results were obtained. If relevant, explain why particular choices were made. Although many elements are listed below, this section should not overwhelm the report. Decisions about which items to address and the level of detail to include should reflect the audience's interests and information needs. Organize this section so that it is clear which indicators, data sources, and methods were used to address each evaluation question. Presenting all three elements in a table may help show clear linkages among them.

☐ **Approach:** Briefly describe the evaluation theories, frameworks, or lenses that informed the evaluation's focus, design, or implementation.

☐ **Evaluation questions:** Identify the questions that framed the evaluation and explain the rationale for their selection.

☐ **Criteria:** If they are not obvious from the evaluation questions, identify the defining characteristics or qualities used to judge the program's performance.

☐ **Indicators:** Identify what was measured for each evaluation question or criterion.

☐ **Data sources:** For each indicator, identify the type and source of information collected—such as individuals, documents, or institutional databases.

☐ **Data source selection:** For each data source, describe how individual cases were chosen—such as through a census or specific sampling techniques.

☐ **Sample size and description:** If sampling was employed, describe how many individual data sources were selected for inclusion in the sample and the actual number from which data were gathered.

☐ **Data collection methods:** Describe how the information was gathered from each data source—such as through interviews, surveys, focus groups, observations, or document review. If mixed methods were used, describe the extent to which and how qualitative and quantitative approaches were integrated.

☐ **Data collection procedures:** Include pertinent procedural information, such as how respondents were invited or encouraged to participate in data collection.

☐ **Instruments:** Identify the tools used to implement each data collection method, such as questionnaires and protocols for interviews, document reviews, focus groups, or observations. Include copies of instruments in appendices if possible. If not, provide a brief description of each instrument. If applicable, discuss how data collectors, coders, or raters were trained or calibrated. Report statistical indicators of reliability and validity, if relevant.

☐ **Timeline:** Identify when each method was implemented and when major evaluation tasks were completed.

☐ **Data management:** Briefly describe how collected data were kept secure and the privacy of individuals was protected.

☐ **Data analysis:** Describe the specific procedures used to organize and transform raw data into findings. Include enough detail so that others could reproduce the analysis for both qualitative and quantitative data. Indicate whether and how multiple data sources or methods were used to measure the same thing.

☐ **Interpretation:** Describe how findings were used to answer the evaluation questions and reach conclusions about the program's quality, value, or importance. Identify who was involved in that process. Include enough detail so that others could reproduce the process and arrive at similar conclusions.

☐ **Limitations:** Describe factors that may have adversely affected the accuracy or credibility of the evaluation results. This should include significant limitations that were within or outside of the evaluation team's control. Include alterative explanation of results, if warranted.

EVALUATION RESULTS

The evaluation results section describes what was learned from the evaluation. While only two items are listed in this checklist, the results section will likely be the longest part of the report, because it includes the most important and substantive information. Organize results by evaluation questions or criteria, rather than data collection methods or sources, to make explicit connections between evaluation questions, conclusions, and findings. For example, *restate each evaluation question* as a heading, and then present findings and conclusions in subsections of each question.

☐ **Findings:** Present the analyzed data and other evidence used to formulate the conclusions. Provide relevant information about the representativeness of the data, such as response rates or data source characteristics.

☐ **Conclusions:** Conclusions are answers to the evaluation questions. Start each conclusion subsection with a statement that directly answers the evaluation question. To enhance transparency, remind the reader of the relevant findings and interpretation procedures used to reach conclusions.

RECOMMENDATIONS

The recommendations section includes suggestions for actions that align with intended evaluation uses. If there are several, group them in categories, such as evaluation question, program component, or timing.

☐ **Development process:** Explain how the recommendations were generated.

☐ **Recommendations for the program:** Identify suggested actions for stakeholders to consider. Refer to the specific evaluation results to support each recommendation. Provide supporting information—such as priorities, timing, and potential costs and benefits—to facilitate action planning.

☐ **Recommendations for future evaluations:** List recommendations for future evaluations of the program, if any. Provide a rationale for each suggestion. This section should be clearly labeled and distinct from evidence-based recommendations about the program.

☐ **Ideas for consideration:** Under certain circumstances, it may be appropriate to include suggestions based on the evaluator's experience, rather than direct evidence. This section should be clearly labeled and distinct from evidence-based recommendations about the program.

REFERENCES

The references section provides information about literature cited in the report, enabling readers to locate sources if desired.

☐ **Sources:** Use a consistent reference style. Provide website addresses for publicly accessible documents.

APPENDICES

Supplementary information that is pertinent to the evaluation, but not critical to readers' understanding of the report, may be included as appendices. Each document included as an appendix should be referenced in the body of the report. The following types of documents may be appropriate for appending to some evaluation reports:

☐ **Data collection materials:** Include data collection instruments and protocols, qualitative coding guides, and blank consent forms.

☐ **List of reviewed documents or artifacts:** List all reviewed artifacts, databases, documents, or other materials, if they were not already mentioned in the methods section. If possible, format the list using the same style used for references. If the information is publicly available, include website addresses or indicate how others can access the materials.

☐ **Supplementary data or findings:** If applicable, include additional data tables that may be of interest to some readers but are not required for understanding the evaluation conclusions. Examples include findings disaggregated by region, social group, or time period. Qualitative data are often analyzed and reported according to thematic categories and the frequency with which those themes appeared in the data. However, some readers may find value in viewing raw qualitative data—those may be included if there is no risk of identifying individual respondents based on their comments.

Resources

This checklist is based on our formal evaluation training and experience conducting evaluations, as well as input from an array of evaluators. In addition, the following resources influenced the content of this checklist, and we recommend them for individuals who would like additional information about determining content for evaluation reports.

Checklist 5: Preparing the Evaluation Report http://bit.ly/ilorep
Developed for evaluation consultants working for the International Labour Organization, this checklist identifies report elements and includes guidance for presenting the information.

Evaluation Report Checklist http://bit.ly/er-miron
This checklist by Gary Miron lists the essential components of an evaluation report and includes a rating scale for assessing completed reports.

Reader-Friendly Writing – 1:3:25 http://bit.ly/chsrfrep
This brief by the Canadian Health Services Research Foundation recommends that reports include a one-page list of main messages, a three-page executive summary, and a report body of up to 25 pages.

Constructing an Evaluation Report http://bit.ly/rep-tips
This brief guide by the U.S. Agency for International Development provides practical tips on the structure, content, and style of evaluation reports.

Evaluation Reporting: A Guide to Help Ensure Use of Evaluation Findings http://bit.ly/cdcrg
This guide by the Centers for Disease Control and Prevention includes advice for enhancing evaluation use by engaging stakeholders, clarifying an evaluation's purpose, and understanding a report's target audience.

Preferred Citation

Robertson, K. N., & Wingate L. A. (2017). *Checklist for program evaluation report content.* Kalamazoo, MI: EvaluATE, The Evaluation Center, Western Michigan University. Retrieved from http://www.evalu-ate.org/resources/checklist-evalrpts/

Acknowledgments

We are indebted to the evaluators who piloted or provided detailed feedback on prior versions of this checklist: Lyssa Becho, Christina Bierring, Martha Brown, Fraser Dalgleish, Melissa Demetrikopoulos, Nora Douglas, Pamela Eddy, Bolaji Fapohunda, Ann Gillard, Andrea Gregg, Aric Gregg, Kylie Hutchinson, Melissa Kovacs, Shelley Maberry, Goldie MacDonald, Nancy Marker, Kathryn Newcomer, Elizabeth Peery, Emma Perk, Cynthia Phillips, Ben Reid, Matthew Roberts, Mike Rudibaugh, Daniela Schroeter, Karen Snyder, Leonard Sterry, Wendy Tackett, Jessica Weitzel, Manjari Wijenaike, and. We are thankful for the useful suggestions provided by attendees at a presentation about an early draft of this checklist: Ruqayyah Abu-Obaid, Dustin Anderson, Chris Coryn, Yu Du, Cheryl Endres, Erica Fiekowsky, Jan Fields, Miranda Lee, Tara Lightner, Will Maddix, Stephen Magura, Mary Ramlow, and Brad Watts. We also appreciate the work Krystin Martens did in laying the foundation for development of this checklist. Any errors or omissions are exclusively our responsibility. Thank you to Cynthia Williams for copyediting.

This material is based upon work supported by the National Science Foundation under Grant No. 1600992. Any opinions, findings, and conclusions or recommendations expressed in this material are those of the authors and do not necessarily reflect the views of the National Science Foundation.

EvaluATE

SUMMARY: Checklist for Program Evaluation Report Content
Kelly N. Robertson and Lori A. Wingate | October 2017

TITLE PAGE
- ☐ Title
- ☐ Recipient(s)
- ☐ Author(s)
- ☐ Date
- ☐ Preferred citation

ACKNOWLEDGMENTS
- ☐ Contributors

TABLE OF CONTENTS
- ☐ Headings
- ☐ Page numbers

LIST OF TABLES AND FIGURES
Include if five or more are in the report.
- ☐ Titles
- ☐ Page numbers

LIST OF ACRONYMS
Include if five or more are in the report.
- ☐ Definitions

EXECUTIVE SUMMARY
- ☐ Most important content (key findings, conclusions, and recommendations)

INTRODUCTION
- ☐ Overview
- ☐ Structure
- ☐ Intended audience
- ☐ Purpose and intended use

PROGRAM DESCRIPTION
- ☐ Goals and/or objectives
- ☐ Funder and funding
- ☐ Organizations involved
- ☐ Intended beneficiaries
- ☐ Program design
- ☐ Context
- ☐ History

EVALUATION BACKGROUND
- ☐ Purpose and intended use
- ☐ Scope
- ☐ Stakeholder engagement
- ☐ Responsiveness to culture and context
- ☐ Budget
- ☐ Evaluation team
- ☐ Prior evaluation

EVALUATION METHODS
Although several items are listed below, this should not be the longest section of the report.
- ☐ Approach
- ☐ Evaluation questions
- ☐ Criteria
- ☐ Indicators
- ☐ Data sources
- ☐ Data source selection (census or sampling)
- ☐ Sample size and description
- ☐ Data collection methods
- ☐ Data collection procedures
- ☐ Instruments
- ☐ Timeline
- ☐ Data management
- ☐ Data analysis
- ☐ Interpretation
- ☐ Limitations

EVALUATION RESULTS
Although only two items are listed below, this section will likely be the longest, because it includes the most important and substantive information. Organize results by evaluation questions or criteria.
- ☐ Findings
- ☐ Conclusions

RECOMMENDATIONS
- ☐ Development process
- ☐ Recommendations for the program
- ☐ Recommendations for future evaluations
- ☐ Ideas for consideration

REFERENCES
- ☐ Sources

APPENDICES
- ☐ Data collection materials
- ☐ List of reviewed documents or artifacts
- ☐ Supplementary data or findings

Visit http://bit.ly/rptchecklist to view the full version of this checklist.

This material is based upon work supported by the National Science Foundation under Grant No. 1600992. Any opinions, findings, and conclusions or recommendations expressed in this material are those of the authors and do not necessarily reflect the views of the National Science Foundation.

Appendix D - Data Cube Template

Community Solutions
Planning & Evaluation
www.communitysolutions.ca

The Reporting Cube

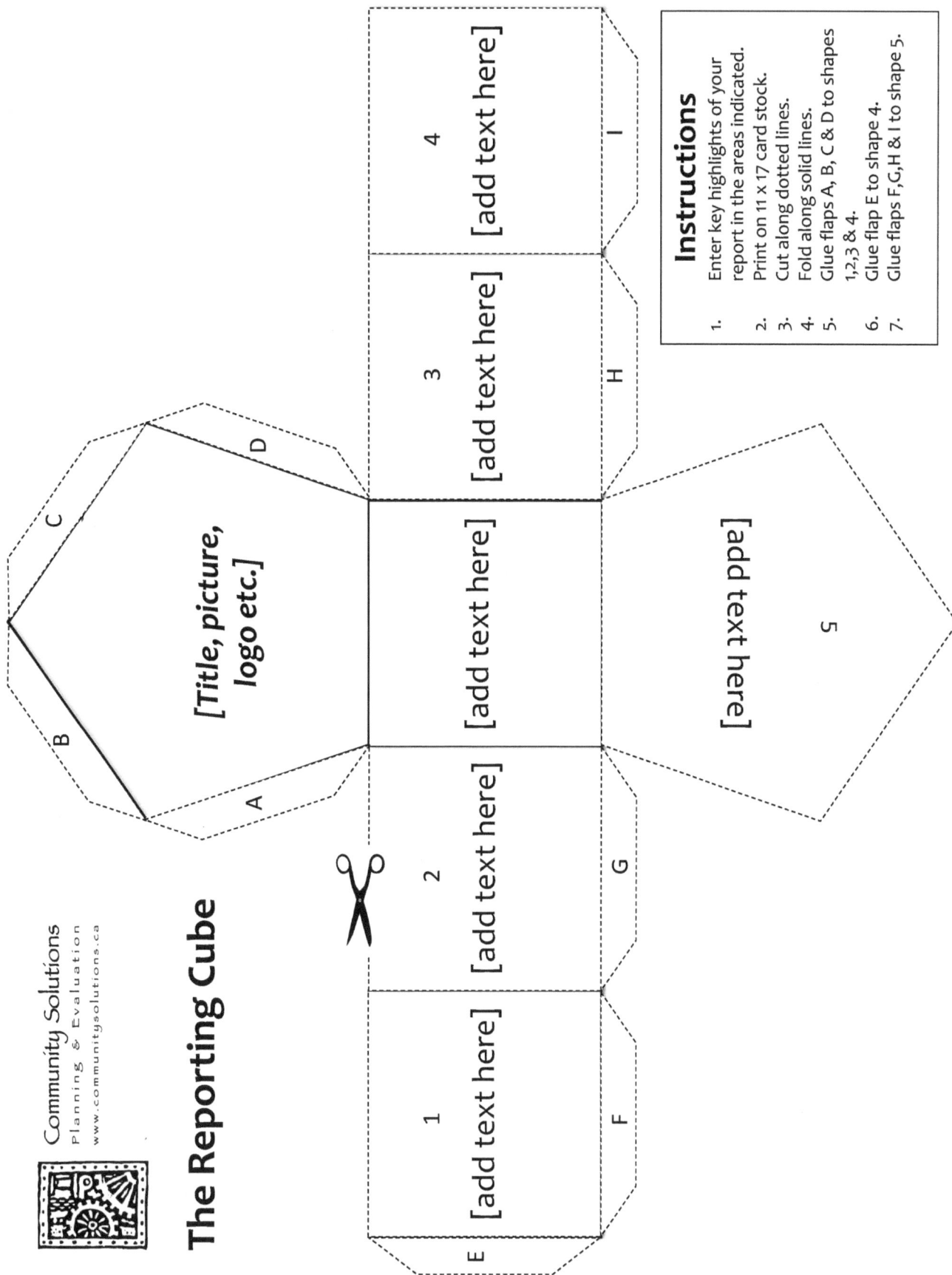

[Title, picture, logo etc.]

A

B

C

D

1 [add text here]

2 [add text here]

3 [add text here]

4 [add text here]

E

F

G

H

I

[add text here]

[add text here]

[add text here]

[add text here]

5 [add text here]

Instructions

1. Enter key highlights of your report in the areas indicated.
2. Print on 11 x 17 card stock.
3. Cut along dotted lines.
4. Fold along solid lines.
5. Glue flaps A, B, C & D to shapes 1,2,3 & 4.
6. Glue flap E to shape 4.
7. Glue flaps F,G,H & I to shape 5.

Bibliography

1. Reynolds, G. (2008). *Presentation Zen: Simple ideas on presentation design and delivery.* Berkeley, CA: New Riders.

2. Avey, P. C. & Desch, M. C. (2013). What do policymakers want from us? Results of a survey of current and former senior National Security decision-makers. *International Studies Quarterly, 58*(4), 227-246.

3. U.S. House of Representatives. (1977). *Final report of the commission on administrative review, Vol. 2 (95th Congress, 1st session).* Washington, DC: Government Printing Office.

4. Silverman, L. (2006). *Wake me up when the data is over: How organizations use stories to drive results.* San Francisco, CA: John Wiley & Sons. Used with permission.

5. Nelson, B. (2012, June 4). *Do you read fast enough to be successful?* Retrieved from http://www.forbes.com/sites/brettnelson/2012/06/04/do-you-read-fast-enough-to-be-successful/#4d37317358f7.

6. Perry, S. (2015, October 5). *1 in 3 Americans lack faith in charities, Chronicle poll finds.* Retrieved from https://www.philanthropy.com/article/1-in-3-Americans-Lacks-Faith/233613.

7. Shawcross, W. (2016, June 28). *Trust in charities is at an all-time low: Time to change.* Retrieved from https://www.theguardian.com/commentisfree/2016/jun/28/trust-charities-low-charitable-work-public.

8. This figure comes from an informal survey that Michael Quinn Patton conducted with evaluators many years ago. It certainly bears out in my own experience and that of the many evaluators I've had in my workshops over the years.

9. Yarbrough, D. B., Shulha, L. M., Hopson, R. K., & Caruthers, F. A. (2011). *The program evaluation standards: A guide for evaluators and evaluation users (3rd ed.).* Thousand Oaks, CA: Sage.

10. Hutchinson, K. (2016). *Survive and thrive: Three steps to securing your program's sustainability.* Vancouver, BC: Community Solutions.

11. Yarbrough, D. B., Shulha, L. M., Hopson, R. K., & Caruthers, F. A. (2011). *The program evaluation standards: A guide for evaluators and evaluation users (3rd ed.).* Thousand Oaks, CA: Sage.

12. Fleischer, D. N. & Christie, C. A. (2009). Evaluation use: Results from a survey of U.S. American Evaluation Association Members. *American Journal of Evaluation, 30*(2), 158-175.

13. Public Profit. (2015). *Dabbling in the data.* Retrieved from http://www.publicprofit.net/Dabbling-In-The-Data.

14. Duarte, N. (2008). *Presenting skills: Know your presentation audience.* Retrieved from http://www.duarte.com/presenting-skills-know-your-presentation-audience/. Used with permission.

15. Reynolds, G. (2008). *Presentation Zen: Simple ideas on presentation design and delivery.* Berkeley, CA: New Riders.

16. Davidson, J. (2007). Editorial: Unlearning some of our social scientist habits. *Journal of MultiDisciplinary Evaluation, 4*(8), iii – vi.

17. Minto, B. (2008). *The pyramid principle.* Upper Saddle River, NJ: Prentice Hall.

18. Gladwell, M. (2000). *The tipping point: How little things can make a big difference.* Boston, MA: Little, Brown and Company.

19. Heath, C. & Heath, D. (2007). *Made to stick: Why some ideas survive and others die.* New York, NY: Random House.

20. Camerer, C. F., Loewenstein, G., & Weber, M. (1989). The curse of knowledge in economic settings: An experimental analysis. *Journal of Political Economy, 97*, 1232-54.

21. Cox, P., Kozak, S., Griep, L., & Moffat, L. (2002). *Splash and ripple: Using outcomes to design and guide community work.* Calgary, AB: PLAN:NET Limited and Health Canada.

22. Mark, S., Moreland, F., & Gage, D. (2006, October 2). *The good food box story.* Vancouver, BC: Edible Strategies Enterprises, Ltd. Used with permission.

23. Medina, J. (2014). *Brain rules.* Seattle, WA: Pear Press.

24. Nickerson, R. S. (1968). A note on long-term recognition memory for pictorial material. *Psychonomic Science, 11*(2), 58.

25. Borkin, M. A., Vo, A. A., Bylinskii, Z., Isola, P., Sunkavalli, S., Oliva, A., & Pfister, H. (2013). What makes a visualization memorable? *IEEE Transactions on Visualization and Computer Graphics, 19*(12), 2306–2315.

26. Borkin, M. A., Bylinskii, Z., Kim, N. W., Bainbridge, C. M., Yeh, C. S., Borkin, D., Pfister, H., & Oliva, A. (2016). Beyond memorability:

Visualization recognition and recall. *IEEE Transactions on Visualization and Computer Graphics*, 22(1), 519-28.

27. Endestad, T. et. al. (2003).Memory for pictures and words following literal and metaphorical decisions. *Imagination, Cognition and Personality*, 23(2,3), 209 – 216.

28. Stenberg, G. (2006). Conceptual and perceptual factors in the picture superiority effect. *European Journal of Cognitive Psychology*, 18(6), 813 – 847.

29. McBride, D. M., & Dosher, A. B. (2002). A comparison of conscious and automatic memory processes for picture and word stimuli: A process dissociation analysis. *Consciousness and Cognition*, 11(3), 423-460.

30. Evergreen, S. (2014). *Presenting data effectively.* Thousand Oaks, CA: Sage.

31. Narain, C. (2006). Total recall. *Nature Neuroscience*, 9, 302.

32. Xu, Y. & Chun, M. M. C. (2006). Dissociable neural mechanisms supporting visual short-term memory for objects. Nature, 440, 91 – 95.

33. Wilairat, N. & EMI Consulting. (2014, April 17). AEA coffee break: *Visualizing findings in executive summaries* [Power Point Slides]. Retrieved from http://comm.eval.org/ coffee_break_webinars/resources/ listofpastwebinarspublic1. Used with permission.

34. Davidson, J. (2007). Editorial: Unlearning some of our social scientist habits. *Journal of MultiDisciplinary Evaluation*, 4(8), iii – vi.

35. Patton, M. Q. (2008). *Utilization-focused evaluation, 4th Ed.* Thousand Oaks, CA: Sage.

36. Evergreen, S. (2014). *Presenting data effectively.* Thousand Oaks, CA: Sage.

37. Evergreen, S. (n.d.). *Potent presentations initiative: Slide design guidelines.* American Evaluation

Association. Retrieved from http:// p2i.eval.org/index.php/slide-design-guidelines/.

38. National Center for Voice and Speech. (n.d.). *Voice qualities.* Retrieved from http://www.ncvs.org/ncvs/ tutorials/voiceprod/tutorial/quality. html.

39. Rivera, E. (2017). *Blast off to stellar slides: 10 strategies to help you design and deliver effective presentations.* Retrieved from http://www.echorivera. com. Used with permission.

40. Office of Performance Evaluations. (2015, February). *The K-12 longitudinal data system (ISEE).* Boise, ID: Idaho Legislature. Retrieved from https:// legislature.idaho.gov/ope/reports/ r1503/. Used with permission.

41. Imagine Canada. (2005). *Evaluation practices in Canadian voluntary organizations.* Retrieved from sourceosbl.ca/sites/default/files/ resources/files/vserp_fact_sheet.pdf. Used with permission.

42. Whiz Kids Workshop. (2014). *Final evaluation.* Used with permission.

43 UBC Faculty of Medicine Evaluation Studies Unit. (2015, May). *E-CLIPs Evaluation Summary.* Used with permission.

44. The Women's and Children's Health Policy Center. (n.d.). *The art and craft of policy briefs: Translating science and engaging stakeholders* [Video file]. Retrieved from http://www.jhsph. edu/research/centers-and-institutes/ womens-and-childrens-health-policy-center/de/policy_brief/video.

45. Duarte, N. (2014). *Spread ideas with effective visual documents.* Retrieved from http://www.duarte.com/ slidedocs/.

46. Emery, A. K. (2016). *The American Evaluation Association in 2020.* Retrieved from: http://www.eval.org/ aeain2020. Used with permission.

47. The Women's and Children's Health Policy Center. (n.d.). *The art and craft of policy briefs: Translating science and engaging stakeholders* [Video file]. Retrieved from http://www.jhsph. edu/research/centers-and-institutes/ womens-and-childrens-health-policy-center/de/policy_brief/video.

48. Global Age Watch. (2014). *Older people count: Making data fit for purpose (Policy brief 4).* Retrieved from http:// www.helpage.org/global-agewatch/ blogs/alex-mihnovits-21956/older-people-count-making-data-fit-for-purpose-760/. Used with permission.

49. Families Together in Albany County. (2006, Winter). *Evaluation update.* Used with permission.

50. Northern California Training Academy. (2006, Spring). *Training Evaluation Update.* Used with permission.

51. Stong, D. R. (2005). *Designing communications for a poster fair.* Pennsylvania State University. Retrieved from: http://www.personal.psu.edu/ drs18/postershow/.

52. Evergreen, S. (n.d.). *Potent presentations initiative: Guidelines for posters.* American Evaluation Association. Retrieved from http://p2i. eval.org/index.php/guidelines_for_ posters/.

53. Hess, G. & L. Liegel. (2008). *Creating effective poster presentations.* Retrieved from: https://projects.ncsu. edu/project/posters/documents/ QuickReferenceV3.pdf.

54. Stong, D. R. (2005). *Designing communications for a poster fair.* Pennsylvania State University. Retrieved from: http://www.personal.psu. edu/drs18/postershow/. Used with permission.

55. Hutchinson, K. (2016). *Survive and thrive: Three steps to securing your program's sustainability.* Vancouver, BC: Community Solutions.

56. Center for Health Progress. (2017, July). *Health perspectives: Hispanics and Latinos.* Retrieved from https://centerforhealthprogress.org/blog/publications/health-perspectives-hispanics-latinos-2/. Used with permission.

57. Wilkerson, S. B. (2017). *10 Steps to Creating an Infographic.* Retrieved from https://magnoliaconsulting.org/tools#infographics. Used with permission.

58. Smith, V. S. (2013). Data dashboard as evaluation and research communication tool. *New Directions in Evaluation*, 140, 21-45.

59. Shapiro, J. (2017, January 13). *Three ways data dashboards can mislead you.* Harvard Business Review. Retrieved from https://hbr.org/2017/01/3-ways-data-dashboards-can-mislead-you.

60. Human Early Learning Partnership. (n.d.). *Coquitlam (SD43) community resources* [map]. Vancouver, BC: University of British Columbia, School of Population and Public Health. Used with permission
For additional maps, please visit http://earlylearning.ubc.ca/maps/edi/.

61. Human Early Learning Partnership. (2016, October). Vancouver (SD39) Wave 6: Vulnerable on one or more scales [map]. In *EDI (Early Years Development Instrument) report.* Vancouver, BC: University of British Columbia, School of Population and Public Health. Retrieved from http://earlylearning.ubc.ca/media/edi_w6_communityprofiles/edi_w6_communityprofile_sd_39.pdf. Used with permission. For additional maps, please visit http://earlylearning.ubc.ca/maps/edi/sd/39/.

62. Norwood, C. (2009). *Making maps that matter? The role of geospatial information in addressing rural landscape change* [Doctoral dissertation]. University of North Carolina, Chapel Hill. Used with permission.

63. The mission of the Learning Dojo is to develop the evidence base for doing development differently in order to create organizational change within USAID. The USAID LEARN Contract supports the Office of Learning, Evaluation and Research in the Bureau for Policy, Planning and Learning at USAID and is managed by Dexis Consulting Group. Used with permission.

64. Parsons, B., Lovato, C., & Hutchinson, K. (2015). *Systems thinking: A way to maximize program effectiveness.* [Video recording]. Retrieved from https://youtu.be/2vojPksdbtI.

65. Metzner, C. & Keene, M. (2011). *Oregon Paint Stewardship Pilot Program.* Retrieved from http://www.paintstewardshipprogram.com. Used with permission.

66. Jordan, J. (2017, July 17). *Email client market share trends for 2017* [Blog post]. Retrieved from https://litmus.com/blog/email-client-market-share-trends-1h-2017.

67. Evergreen, S. (2013). *Findings cookies* [Blog post]. Retrieved http://stephanieevergreen.com/findings-cookies/. Used with permission.

68. Evergreen, S. (2013). *Scratch-off graphs* [Blog post]. Retrieved from http://stephanieevergreen.com/scratch-off-graphs/. Used with permission.

69. UBC Learning Exchange. (2017, May). *Voices UP! Puppet Scene Rehearsal.* Vancouver, BC.

70. American Dance Therapy Association & Furcron, C. (2014, May). *Dance: Positively changing lives of urban youth* [Video]. Atlanta, GA: American Dance Therapy Association (www.adta.org). Retrieved from https://www.youtube.com/watch?v=la3ohS7GZOA. Used with permission.

71. Rogers, E. M. (2003). *Diffusion of innovations, 5th Ed.* New York, NY: The Free Press.

72. Moore, G. (1991). *Crossing the chasm.* New York, NY: Harper Collins. Used with permission.

www.ingramcontent.com/pod-product-compliance
Lightning Source LLC
Chambersburg PA
CBHW041447210326
41599CB00004B/162